A KINGDOM FAR AWAY

KARI GUSSO

WISE INK CREATIVE PUBLISHING

MINNEAPOLIS

ISBN 13: 978-1-63489-133-2
Printed in the United States of America
First Printing: 2018

22   21   20   19   18   5   4   3   2   1

Cover design by Emily Rodvold
Interior design by Patrick Maloney

WISE Ink
CREATIVE ★ PUBLISHING
837 Glenwood Ave.
Minneapolis, MN 55405
www.wiseinkpub.com

PROLOGUE

2000

I was sweating, wearing only a long T-shirt. I walked back and forth from the living room to the hallway with a slight bounce in each step. Lauren was screaming. She was only about two weeks old—pretty good during the day, but about four o'clock, she lost it. She fussed and worked herself into a full-on screaming fit. The crying would last until about ten. *Are babies always this fussy?* I thought. I'd babysat when I was a teen, but I couldn't remember the kids crying this much. Night after night, I walked back and forth. Sometimes I caught a glimpse of myself and Lauren in the mirror. *She's so little*, I thought. Even with the screaming, I managed a smile. I started singing her a song. It was just her name, sung to the tune of a lullaby. She loved hearing her name. This song was one of the few things that would calm her down.

"Mom, I know it would be fun to go out," I said. I tried to explain to her how difficult every night was, when Lauren screamed and screamed. I didn't think a babysitter could handle her crying; I thought they would hurt her.

"I want you and Jared to go out and have a nice dinner. Dad and I will stay here, and Lauren will be okay," my mom said.

Okay, I thought, *Mom knows what she is doing; she raised us three girls.* I put on jeans and a new shirt, put my hair in a ponytail, and—the big kicker of the night—applied some lip gloss.

"You're going all out," Jared said, laughing.

"Hey, this is as good as it's gonna get." I winked.

The night was peaceful. Halloween season was upon us, and the trees were starting to change. We talked about what Lauren should be for Halloween. "She can help me hand out candy," I said as we walked to the car.

"We'll have to play it by ear," Jared said as he scrunched up his nose. "Night is not her favorite time of day."

We drove into the garage. I missed Lauren so much. I couldn't wait to see her. My dad met us at the door. "Shhhhh!" he said. "Don't wake up Lauren! Don't move, don't walk, don't breathe."

I smiled. "That bad? How did the night go?"

My mom was sitting in the recliner, rocking little Lauren. "Kari," she whispered. "You cannot leave this baby with a babysitter. I don't know what you and Jared are going to do." She looked exhausted.

"It's tough," I said. "We know she's a little pistol."

"I'm so sorry. I didn't realize it was this bad," Mom said disappointedly.

I looked at Jared and shrugged my shoulders. *It has to get better, right?*

CHAPTER 1

LAUREN SLAMMED HER HEAD against the tiled bathroom wall.

"Lauren, stop!" I yelled, trying to hold her still. Her head hitting the wall was like a bowling ball hitting the floor. It sent chills up my spine. Jared was sitting on Lauren's hospital bed. I looked up at him with an expression of "*What the hell am I supposed to do?*"

Lauren took a swing at me. "Don't you dare," I said to her in a sharp tone.

She backed off and looked at me with her big, sad, brown eyes. "Mommy, don't leave me. I love you. I don't want to stay here."

Tears streamed down my face, soaking my shirt. My gut ached for our firstborn child. She wasn't given a say in the matter. She was born with a mental illness. She was trapped in her body, trying to figure out her emotions.

Lauren took the cap off the shampoo bottle. *What is she going to do?* I thought. She started to viciously rub it against her hand. "Honey, stop!" I said. She continued, and I couldn't get the cap out of her hand.

"Go away! I hate you. You're a bitch. You suck."

I looked at Jared and saw the sadness and anger in his eyes as he watched me take the abuse. Lauren was in full throttle on one of her many "meltdowns," as we called them.

The nurse came in the room. "Kari, can we get some of the paperwork done for Lauren's admission?" she asked.

"No!" Lauren started screaming and crying. "I don't want to stay. Mommy, don't leave me."

I was finally able to take the cap from her clenched fist. I gave the lid to the nurse as I walked out of Lauren's room. Lauren followed me out, Jared and the nurse behind her. The other adolescents were getting ready for bed. *This place is always busy*, I thought. *So many kids have to endure the grip of mental health.* The nurse put us in a small conference room. It was hot, and with all the doors locked, I felt like I was in jail. This was Lauren's ninth stay in the mental health unit, so I was familiar with the admission process. Lauren continued to rant, cry, and holler. I looked around and saw the staff roaming like lions getting ready to attack their prey.

"I think we need to remove Lauren from the room," a nurse said sternly.

Even I'm *afraid of these people*, I thought. I wanted to be at home watching TV and eating popcorn. I was so angry at the hand I was dealt, and more so on Lauren's behalf. A guard cop showed up at the door. *Man, here we go.* I put my head down on the table and cried harder.

"No, I'm not leaving, asshole," said Lauren. "You can't take me. Stop, you're hurting me! Mommy, please, I want to stay with you."

I looked deep into Lauren's eyes. I saw a child in anguish. All I could do was sit and wait for them to take her out of the conference room. I knew that was what I needed to do. "I'm a terrible mom. Why am I doing this? I want to take her home and put her to bed and sit and rub her back," I told Jared as I sobbed. I wanted to ignore what was going on; maybe it would go away. I wanted to keep her safe myself, but I knew that I couldn't. I felt like I was losing my grip on my life preserver, and I was slowly sinking.

Jared looked at me with big eyes. "Are you crazy? We can't handle her at home!"

Deep down, I knew that. She wouldn't be safe. Nikki and Megan wouldn't be safe. My gut twisted and turned and my head spun. I felt out of control. I felt like I was in a movie watching somebody else's life. *Where did I go wrong? I had to have done something to cause this,* I thought as I rubbed my temples. We continued to fill out the paperwork. One would think they would keep this information on file so I could sign something stating that nothing had changed in the six months since she was last admitted. There were about fifteen pages to fill out. The hospital wanted information like *How does your child learn best?* and *What are three positive things about your child that will help us get to know her better?* I didn't think anyone read this crap—at least, they hadn't in the last eight admissions. "She learns best while wearing yellow rubber boots," I wrote. I laughed out loud. *Huh, we'll see if they notice.*

I sat slumped in my chair with a damp tissue in my hand. *I know admission to this hospital is a means to keep her safe.* Although, really, they were a glorified babysitter. For the first few admissions, I was hopeful that they would figure things out. We needed help. I was so naive. I was crushed when I realized it didn't work that way.

I finished filling out the papers. Jared and I signed what we needed to sign.

"I'm not watching that admissions video again," I said snottily, like it was their fault she was here. I could see Lauren walking back and forth in front of the closed door, pacing like an animal in a cage. I felt like I was going to throw up. I was so pissed and sad at the same time. "I don't want to have to put her through this again," I said to Jared.

"I know." He took my hand, and we walked out onto the big, open unit. There were about fifteen rooms that lined the perimeter of the adolescents' ward. The kids were all between thirteen and eighteen and required hospitalization for mental health. They were all standing in their doorways. From past hospitalizations, I'd learned that when it was room time they were not to come out of their rooms; if this rule were broken, there would be consequences. The kids stared at us. I wanted to give each and every one of them a hug and tell them that it would be okay. That they weren't at fault for whatever mental health issues they were cursed with.

Lauren was holding on to me for dear life. She was five-foot-nine, two hundred pounds, and sixteen years old, growing into a mature adult woman.

"Lauren, Daddy and I need to leave now. You'll be okay; we'll come back tomorrow." I had said those words countless times.

"No, please don't leave. I love you. I won't be naughty, I promise."

My chest hurt like my heart was being ripped out of my body. "You're not naughty, Lauren," I said, sniffling. I don't think she heard me. She was never naughty; she was being admitted because she tried to harm herself by cutting up her arm. I wanted to take this burden from her so badly. She felt so mentally unstable that to her dying was the only answer. "Lauren, wanting to die is not being naughty," I whispered.

I was trying to hold it together, but I was failing. My mouth was dry, and I couldn't form words. I felt like a freshman trying to give a speech to the whole school. "I gotta go, honey," I managed to get out.

"No, Mommy!" The guard and a larger male nurse came and took hold of Lauren's arms and pulled her away from me. Every piece of tissue in my body hurt. I was crying out loud like a toddler.

"Stop fighting us, Lauren, or we'll put you in the Chair," the big man said sternly. The Chair was something they used to restrain the kids' hands. That was it; I lost it. I wanted my kid back. *I can't leave*, I thought. *They're going to hurt her.* Before I could move toward her, I was picked up by a staff member and my husband. I was taken outside the locked unit.

As the door clicked shut I could hear my baby screaming, "No, don't do that! You're hurting me! Mommy, help me."

I was broken. Broken into many pieces. "God, why?" I said. I cried and cried until my stomach hurt and my head was pounding. I walked in the door and went to my room, straight into my closet. Lying on the floor in the dark, I curled into a fetal position. *Someday she will be safe and happy. She won't be trapped anywhere. She will be safe with no mental health issues, happy and laughing, having fun with no worries in the world. Not the world we know of, but the world we wait for. A kingdom promised to us, far away.*

CHAPTER 2

"Thanks, Krystal, for all your help. I know you had some pull in that decision," I said. We were walking out together from an IEP—Individualized Education Program—meeting with the school district. I visited with Krystal on the way out. "I hate this; it's so frustrating," I said to her.

Lauren was a junior and only had four credits. *What the heck is she going to do without a high school degree?* I thought. *I can't even get her to stay in the building without a catastrophe.*

Krystal was a good friend. She leaned in and gave me a big hug. "Kari, we all want Lauren to succeed. If we can't help her here, then we need to find someone somewhere who can," she said. "I think Brooks will be an excellent school for her. They specialize in kids with autism and can deal with emotional outbursts. They also work with students with learning disabilities." I wiped the tears from my eyes.

"Kari, you ready to go?" Jeff and Samantha, our education attorneys, were standing with Jared. Samantha was carrying boxes of

Lauren's medical and school records.

"Those must be getting heavy," I said, grabbing a box. I continued to walk with the attorneys and Jared out to the car. I turned around to see Krystal standing next to the superintendent. I gave a quick, friendly wave. "He makes me nervous," I whispered. But he seemed like a caring man underneath all the superiority. I could see it in his eyes at the meeting; he finally understood the complexity of Lauren's disease. I took a deep breath.

"That went well," Jeff said. "They were much more responsive than I thought they would be, very easy to work with." Jeff and Samantha were well known in Minneapolis, and we needed them in our case. Our school district couldn't support Lauren's needs, but I wasn't going to give up on her; we needed to figure out plan B. She needed a school that could support her mental and academic needs. Brooks Academy in Illinois seemed to have what Lauren needed.

"I'm relieved the school district agreed to pay this time. Those private schools that offer specialized care for emotional and learning disabilities are very expensive."

Jared cleared his throat. "You got that right. We went through that song and dance with the last school placement. I paid over 100K out of pocket." Jared shook Jeff's hand. "Thanks for all your help."

I shook Samantha's hand and ended up giving her a hug. "We'll be in touch," she said. "Let us know how she does."

"Will do," I said as I waved from the open car window.

Jared and I looked at each other. I was exhausted. "At least we have the school district backing us," Jared said. "It took some work, but I think they finally see the big picture now." Lauren was going to be a junior and hadn't been in school full time for about three years. She had been in and out of programs as we tried to figure out what was going on. I was so tired of constantly fighting for someone to help. I put my feet on the dash and stared out the window blankly, thinking about how horrible the last placement was.

CHAPTER 3

SIX MONTHS EARLIER

WE WERE JUST COMING off summer break, trying to think of different educational options. We enrolled Lauren at Carver, which was in a larger school district. Our town neighbored the Carver district, and we thought it could offer Lauren special education and emotional support at a higher level. After meeting with an education team, it was decided that the Carver-Flynn building would be the best fit for her, as they had an emotional and behavioral program.

Lauren was very excited and nervous to start at the new school. "Don't I go to Carver?" she said, confused.

"I thought so," I said, contemplating the new arrangement. "They must have moved some things around, and now your special school is at the Carver-Flynn site."

"Oh, okay." Lauren was satisfied with that answer.

I sat down at the kitchen table, ran my fingers through my hair, and thought, *This school needs to work. I'm running out of options.*

The small school bus picked her up at our house. I was so pleased that they had bus service. I still needed to get Megan and Nikki to school. Jared and I usually divided and conquered, as we said. "I'll get Lauren on the bus and then drive Nikki to school," I explained to Jared. "Megan, grab your backpack and get in Dad's car," I said, loading the breakfast dishes in the dishwasher. "I work today at Dr. Dillon's office, so I should be home before Dad. You guys start your homework when you get home, please."

"Whatever," Lauren said.

I looked at Megan and Nikki, hoping what I said was not in vain. "Please," I said with a pouty lip. They started laughing. "Lauren, the bus is here. Have a good day and try to make this work. I love you." I waved at the bus.

"What is Lauren going to do on the bus?" Nikki asked. "I hope she doesn't get in a fight."

Blunt honesty, I thought. *Only from the mouth of a child.* "Me too," I answered her. "She'll listen to her earbuds." I could see her pressing one into her ear before the bus drove off.

I SAT ON THE counter at the office, visiting with the other nurses. We didn't have any patients yet. We got the scoop on everyone's lives; it kept us sane. "I hope this school works," I said. "They seem to have the program that she needs. It should be a great fit for her." I was hoping to sound optimistic.

The first patient walked in, and I jumped off the counter. "Hi, Allie," I said. "How are you? I'll take you to the exam room now." *I feel sick. Something is off*, I thought as I walked Allie to the room. I was in a good mood, but I had a sense of impending doom. I was always so anxious when Lauren was at school or out with her peers. I felt like I was waiting for the phone to ring, for someone to give me bad news. Today I knew I was not 100 percent of what I could have been as a nurse; there was just too much on my mind.

Every day, the same thing, worry all day. I grabbed my purse and took a clonazepam. *This will take away the anxiety*, I thought and went to work.

Days passed, and Lauren was doing okay. A few hiccups here and there. "I wish she liked school more," I told the gals at the office over coffee one morning. "She hates authority and being told what to do. That makes being a kid in our society a little tough." I rolled my eyes. "She flat-out refuses to do homework. I have to drive her to school now because she is scared."

"What is she scared of?" Lori asked.

"I don't know; she said the teachers were mean and yelled at her. They want her to do all of these classes online. How is she going to follow along on the computer when she can't follow a live teacher?" I gritted my teeth.

"I'm sorry, Kari," Lucy said. "That has got to be tough." I grabbed another clonazepam to settle my nerves.

"Kari, your cell phone is ringing," Dotty said.

Crap, I hope it's not the school, I prayed. I was just waiting for the other shoe to drop. I looked at my phone like I was looking at a test score. My stomach fell. I nodded to Dotty and went outside to talk. She gave me the don't-be-too-long-we're-busy look. I knew Dotty was genuinely concerned about my situation, but I also knew the frustration of being down a nurse. The office could get really hectic when one of us was missing.

"Mrs. Gusso," the woman on the phone said.

"Yes, this is her," I answered.

"This is Melva, the principal at Carver-Flynn. We have had an incident that involved Lauren."

My stomach fell, and I felt like I was going to throw up. I shook my head. "What?" I said, my mouth so dry my tongue wouldn't even work.

"Lauren was disrespectful to the teachers, so they sent her to my office. I visited with Lauren and told her this was not acceptable and that there were going to be consequences. She's in detention now. She has to stay inside when the others go out, and she will sit in a cubby in the corner by herself so that she is not disrespectful to anyone else."

I tried to comprehend what she was saying. "Okay, I will talk to her tonight. Thanks for calling." I walked back into the office. I smiled at the next patient, drew blood, and assisted with procedures. I had learned that, when I got stressed, I blocked out thoughts and emotions to get through the day. When I got phone calls about Lauren, I had a hard time concentrating on the matter at hand. The staff was getting annoyed with all the interruptions, but I didn't know what to do.

I walked into the nurses' station, where I stood and stared blankly. My mind was mush. I muscled through the day, quiet, doing what I needed to do. I thought, *I probably come across as antisocial,* but I didn't want to talk to anyone. I shut off my computer, gathered my stuff, and walked to my car. I decided to call the school for more information.

"Hi, Julie." I took a deep breath. "I was wondering if I could get more information about Lauren and today." Julie was Lauren's counselor at Carver-Flynn. She was very nice, but she was twenty-four and had no experience working with high-risk, mentally ill kids.

"Hey Kari, I'm glad you called. Lauren was struggling with staying on the computer and doing her work. We talked to her about staying on task, and she was not respectful."

"How long does she need to be on the computer?"

"Well, all day," she said matter-of-factly. "All of our classes are online." I was so confused; I was never told that she would be on a computer all day.

Silence.

"Julie, I'm very frustrated. I feel that there is no program or protocol for students like Lauren."

Again, silence.

I started sweating and a headache came on instantly. "Julie," I said, trying not to sound too bitchy, "Lauren has ADHD, autism, a learning disability, and severe anxiety—all noted on her IEP. She can maintain focus on a computer for half an hour max, and that is with assistance. There is no way she is going to stay focused for eight hours."

"Well, that is how we do it here."

"What about her IEP? Her testing, scores, and interventions that are supposed to help her?" I felt like I was talking to a wall. "Can I talk to Melva?" I asked, frustrated. I waited on hold for a minute or two, listening to the elevator music.

"This is Melva." She sounded defensive. I explained that I was updated on what had happened today. Bothered, she said, "There is no reason Lauren cannot work on the computer by herself. We have people that are available to help her; she just has to ask for help." I wanted to bang my head on the dash.

"Melva, we talked about this at our last IEP meeting. She's not going to ask for help. She sits and gets agitated when she is having an issue, and then she slowly starts to spiral. In her IEP, she has guidelines for your teachers to follow. Why are these not being followed?"

"Well, not all the teachers have access to the IEP," she said.

"What?" I said. "Surely I misheard you. How do they know how to help her?"

She snapped back at me: "The IEP is private information. Not everyone can see it; they don't have access."

I tried to stay calm. "Again, how do they know how to help

Lauren?"

Melva talked in circles, and I never really got an answer regarding the IEP. "Lauren will have detention tomorrow and Friday," she said, ending the conversation.

I was heated. I didn't even know what to do with the information. I decided to call the district's director of special ed. I got her voicemail. I left a message about my conversation with Melva and my concern about Lauren's IEP.

At home, I walked in the door mentally exhausted from the day. "Jared, I don't understand how they can't read her IEP. It's like not following the recipe and getting mad when your cake doesn't look like the picture." I knew Jared agreed with me.

"Call and set up an IEP meeting, and we can discuss it," he said, frustrated.

"I'm really getting tired of having to advocate for Lauren in every school we are in. Why isn't there a standard for all kids who have emotional and behavioral issues? Mental health is so underestimated in school. They're treated like criminals. Last time I checked, it was not a crime to have a mental illness." I fell on the bed face first and screamed into my pillow.

Later that night, I got a voicemail from the director of special ed. She said I could only work with Melva, the principal, and that she was not getting involved. I didn't know if I should laugh or cry.

The next morning on the way to school, I talked to Lauren to help reduce her anxiety. "Lauren, just try to get through the next couple of days and do what they say," I said. "Detention won't last too long—two days, she said." I tried to give her the idea that we were behind the teachers, even though that was far from the truth.

"Okay, Mom, I'll try. But they're mean. I ask for help, and they tell me to read the directions or try harder. I can't try harder, Mom."

"Lauren, just do your best." She got out of the car and walked into the school.

These few days were a giant struggle for Lauren; she did not do well with consequences, but she muscled through and was able to serve the detention. She had a goal, and she achieved it. I was on pins and needles all week. Thank goodness it was Friday.

"Mom, I don't want you and Dad to go on your trip," Lauren said as she was setting the table for dinner.

"Lauren, Grandma and Grandpa are staying with you. They'll take care of you, Megan, and Nikki. They've stayed with you guys many times before, and they live half a mile from us. It's not like we're leaving you with strangers. On Monday you'll be back in school, and the time will fly by."

"When does your boat leave?" Nikki asked.

"Monday," I said. "So Dad and I are going to leave tomorrow. We will be home in less than a week. Everything will be okay, I promise."

Everyone has a happy place, and my happy place is a Carnival Cruise in the Caribbean with the best boy band in the world. I am what they call a Blockhead. New Kids on the Block has given me and the rest of their now-adult fans an annual opportunity to relive the craze that exploded in 1989. Every year, my inner thirteen-year-old comes out as we relax and enjoy NKOTB for four days. Everyone giggles and pokes fun at me for going, but I have the time of my life.

We flew to New Orleans and met up with other cruise-goers. I was so happy we got this chance to be a couple for five days. We needed it. Our life had been so crazy.

I turned to talk to Jared; my face hurt from laughing. I loved seeing all the return cruise-goers from the last seven years. Elated, I said to Jared, "I can't believe how many awesome people are on this boat—literally friends for a lifetime." I loved watching the crazy fans too. Believe me, there are some crazy-obsessed people. I'd looked forward to this week all year.

"When we get on the lido deck for sail-away party, I'll call my mom and dad quick and tell them we're shutting phones off over international waters," Jared said.

Screams were everywhere. "Hey, Kari! How are you?" I heard in an Australian accent—it was my good friend Agnus, who'd come from all the way across the world for this cruise. I hugged Agnus—we laughed and talked a mile a minute.

"I'm so happy we're all here. How was your flight?" While we were catching up, Jared looked at his phone, then looked at me.

I crooked my head. "You have got to be kidding," I said, deflated.

"Hello," Jared said. He talked for a few minutes and then motioned to me that he was walking back to the room, where he could have a private conversation.

"Is everything okay?" I asked.

"No." He frowned and walked away. My happy balloon burst at that moment, and we weren't even at sea yet. My excitement, squashed. I saw all these people starting to celebrate the next four days. I was standing on the lido deck looking at the big sky. I felt like a five-year-old who'd lost her mom in the store, completely overwhelmed with anxiety and fear. I was so tired of always being blasted with something. I just wanted to go somewhere and do something without the constant fear that my phone would ring.

I sat and looked at the water as the huge boat started to move, watching the water churn below. *It looks like my stomach feels. What happened?* I wondered. We were well into the sail-away party, and I kept looking for Jared. I was getting more worried the longer he was gone. Finally, I saw him walk onto the deck. He saw me, and I waved. He motioned for me to come to him. I let our friends know that we would be right back. They knew something was wrong.

"What is going on?" I asked in a total panic. We walked back to our room, which was on deck 10, very close to the lido deck.

"That was Dad. Apparently Lauren had a rough day."

"What happened?" I asked—but I didn't want to know.

"The morning went well. Dad said all the girls were in good moods. Mom dropped Lauren off at school, and she walked in, no problem. But apparently, when Lauren walked in the door, one of the teachers said to her, 'You have detention again today.'"

"But it's Monday. Her detention was on Friday," I interrupted. He looked at me with frustration. "Yes," Jared said. "And this, of course, made Lauren very anxious." Then he told me what happened.

"Lauren was very upset when they told her that she still had detention. Apparently she asked what she did and was told to take her seat in class. After that she was more anxious and wanted to go in the hall or get fresh air. Her anxiety was amping up, as we know it does, and she told one of the teachers that she was feeling like harming herself."

"Well yeah," I said, "we've taught Lauren to verbalize what her feelings and emotions are to avoid the self-harm."

Jared nodded and continued. "I guess she asked to talk to Grandma Cee, and they said no. It sounds like she wanted fresh air, walked up to the door, and put her hand on the knob to open the door. They thought she was going to run away."

My stomach fell. "What happened?" I asked, not really wanting to know.

"I guess they restrained her. She told Grandpa Ned that they pushed her to the ground and held her there."

I imagined Lauren there, scared and crying.

"She was able to get a drink of water after she calmed down."

"How is she now?" Jared gave me a look. "There's more?" I asked, mortified.

"She must have thought that one of the teachers was going to hurt her. I guess after her drink of water at the water fountain someone took her arm and was going to lead her to class. She pushed them away. In doing that, apparently she hit the teacher in the head."

I sat down on the bed next to the cute little towel animal that the cruise attendants made for fun. I wanted to throw it overboard.

"I guess the teacher decided to press charges, because the police are involved. I'm not exactly sure about what happened next, but Lauren was put in an office to contain her and she opened the window and jumped out and ran. She has some small cuts and bruises from that. She said she thought she was going to jail for assault, which is what they told her. She was terrified."

She doesn't even know what that is, I thought, getting more pissed.

"Grandpa Ned said she was standing by the cop car when he got there. He was upset because they had her in cuffs and Lauren was a mess. He said, 'She's autistic and has some special needs. Why are they treating her that way?'" Jared smiled. "I think the officer asked the staff if that was true, and they all looked at each other. Then the officer told Grandpa to take Lauren home and that there would be no charges. Well, those shitheads, they have no idea what they are doing."

"Now what?"

"Grandpa Ned said he will keep her home this week."

I was exhausted. So much for a carefree vacation. Jared took my hand, and we walked to the lido deck sail-away party.

The boat left port, and we had a good time, but the spark in my soul was out. *Why does everything have to suck all the time?* I thought. I felt overwhelmed, sad, and scared, but nobody on the boat realized it. I hid it well. I could have told them, but I didn't even know where I would start. Jared and I must have seemed distant on that cruise. Some even mentioned how rude they thought Jared was because he wasn't talking. He just did not have anything to say. The cruise ended and we flew home, back to the craziness of reality.

Lauren had a really hard time engaging again at Carver-Flynn from that point on. "Lauren, you have to go to school," I pleaded.

"I'm not going; they're assholes." Lauren stayed put in the front seat of the car.

A staff member knocked on the window. "Lauren, do you want to come in and try school?"

Lauren shook her head. "You're mean. Why would I go in there with you? I hate you."

I held the steering wheel, perplexed and clueless as to what I should do. I didn't want her to be restrained, and I didn't feel that this was a good place for her—I felt like this school was more for juvenile detention than for mental health assistance, and Lauren was not a criminal. But I knew she had to go to school. "I guess we'll go home and try again tomorrow," I said.

Day in and day out, school or home, the days got to be long. Lauren was bored, and I was tired of keeping her busy. "I can't get her to stay at the school; she has a complete anxiety attack if I leave," I told Krystal. "I can't believe that the state of South Dakota doesn't have a better handle on these types of cases. I shouldn't have to be fighting this fight. Other states have classes, departments, and policies in place for students that suffer from emotional and behavioral issues. We need to start looking at different options. She won't do any schoolwork; she is so far behind. I can't even get her to make her bed or walk the dogs. I'm at a loss. I don't know what to do. We need some help."

A few days later, Jared and I pulled into the parking lot of

Carver-Flynn. I hated meeting like this, but I was so angry with the staff. "I'm glad they are showing us the surveillance video from that day," Jared said.

"I'm scared to see it," I said quietly. "I'm not sure what I will do when I see them hurting her."

"They can start explaining their actions," Jared said sternly.

As we arrived at the school, we were escorted to a very warm boardroom. "I don't want another kid to experience this," I explained to the staff. "This is not acceptable. Not every mental health disorder is a cookie-cutter copy from person to person. As a nurse, I see many patients come through the hospital door. When you come across a very independent sixteen-year-old with diabetes who has low blood sugar because he refused to eat after his football game, you don't throw him in the hospital and isolate him from his family and restrain him when his blood sugar doesn't regulate. You certainly don't tell him it's all his fault and that he needs to knock it off. That's what I feel like I am dealing with." I was so hot. "This room is so damn stuffy," I said, but continued my rant. "Mental health is so misunderstood. These kids are not trying to act out; they need love, understanding, compassion, and training to help them overcome their disease, not jail and restraints, medications and police."

Lauren never went back to Carver-Flynn after that day.

I BUMPED MY ARM on the dash as the car hit a pothole.

"Oh, sorry," Jared said. "Are you okay, hon?"

I focused on the here and now, glad to be done with Carver-Flynn. "I was just thinking," I answered. "I'm happy Lauren is going to Brooks." I smiled and looked out the window.

CHAPTER 4

"Mom, where's my purple jacket?" Lauren yelled from her room.

"It's in your closet," I hollered back.

"Where's my backpack, the one we got a few weeks ago?"

I rolled my eyes and calmly walked to her room. "Lauren, it's in the laundry room, where it's always kept."

"Oh, okay. Sorry, Mom, I didn't know."

She says she is sorry and that she doesn't know? I swear she's playing me. "We're leaving in fifteen minutes!" I shouted. Looking at Jared, I repeated the itinerary for the next few days: "We're flying to St. Louis, renting a car, and driving to Carbondale, Illinois. Lauren will stay with me in the hotel. I'll help her get her dorm set up, and I'll be home in a few days."

Megan and Nikki were sitting at the breakfast bar. "Mommy, why do you have to go?" Nikki said in between sips of milk. "I'll miss you."

"She has to go to Lauren's school again to move her in *again*." Megan looked at me with a half grin, half frown. My stomach started to hurt.

"I know, you guys. I need to do this for Lauren. She needs assistance. She can't do this alone. I will be home in a few days."

Megan got up from the table. "But *I* get to go to school and do all my stuff alone, with you not here." I saw a tear in her eye. She walked downstairs. Nikki continued to eat her cereal.

I was so frustrated that Lauren couldn't go to a school near us. My eyes started to tear up. I was always torn between Jared, Nikki, Megan, and Lauren—where I should be, who should be my priority. They say love multiplies. Love does not multiply; you are forced to divide it up among family members.

"I'm walking out the door," I said sadly.

Jared came behind me and gave me a hug. "It will be fine. Nikki and Megan are fine. I'm here with them." He was very forthright. "You get Lauren squared away."

I looked at him with teary eyes. "How am I so lucky to have such a wonderful husband?"

He kissed my cheek. "Do you have everything you need?" he asked.

"I'll have to go to the store when we get to Carbondale and get most of what she needs. I can't pack all that stuff and haul it there on an airplane," I said, knowing the response I would get from him.

"Just don't go crazy and spend too much money, okay?" He winked at me.

I was right, I thought. Lauren hopped in the car with Milo, our dog, in tow. Brooks Academy agreed to let Lauren bring Milo—a very sweet, well-behaved golden doodle. "I can't believe we're bringing Milo," I said to Lauren. I shook my head.

"He's my dog, Mom, and he helps me feel safe," Lauren said as she petted the top of Milo's head. Milo had a certification as a therapy dog; we were slowly working on the service dog portion. There was no legal certification for service dogs at this time. It was all subjective and up to the owner how they trained the dog. Dogs for hearing, blindness, and other major health issues were in a different category and were trained very well by professionals. Milo was allowed to fly at Lauren's side, as he was her therapy dog. However, he was not a fan of flying. Milo was very excited when he could get off the plane and find a pet relief station. He was probably thinking, *Finally, we're able to get out of that strange box we were riding in.*

"Mom, grab Milo's leg. Pull on his collar—no, just pick him up." I laughed as I tried to stay standing on the escalator with a rolling bag in one hand and Milo now in the other. Milo was not entirely sure he liked this ride either. I had visions of his hair getting stuck in the escalator, so I was holding the dog like an infant.

"Lauren, we need to use the elevator from now on," I said breathlessly. "Go to the left. Let's get the car."

I was relieved my phone had GPS. *What did people do back when there were no smartphones?* I asked myself. I plugged in Carbondale, Illinois. Two and a half hours. Lauren was excited, smiling and looking at her phone. Milo crashed in the backseat, exhausted from being stressed for the last four hours on an airplane.

The weather was hot, sticky, and humid. We drove through parts of Illinois and Missouri. There were tons of corn and beans and beans and corn. I felt sleepy in the hot sun. Finally, we pulled up to Brooks Academy. It was a nice-looking school. There were seven buildings: separate dorms for boys and girls, a big gym, a cafeteria, the school building, an admissions building, and a nursing building. There was a large parking lot that doubled for a basketball court and a hangout area when school was out for the day. Lots of grassy areas to play ball or lay out in the sun. We had toured

Brooks Academy about a month ago, so we knew where to go to meet the staff.

"Let's see who's here," I said. I pulled up to the dorm Lauren would be staying in, and a few girls came out to greet us. Milo needed to get out and run.

"Hi, I'm Tricia," one of the girls said.

Lauren looked at her. "Say hi, Lauren," I urged.

"Hi, I'm Lauren."

"Is this your dog? Oh my gosh, he is so cute," Tricia said in a high-pitched squeal. Just then about twenty students came running up to see Milo.

Relieved, I thought, *This is one of the reasons Milo is right for Lauren.* Lauren was so socially awkward, and Milo acted as a buffer, gave her something to talk about, and gave others something to ask her about. I was hopeful; maybe Brooks would be a good fit for her. *Please, please provide these girls with patience to understand Lauren, and please help Lauren understand them. Help them form a healthy friendship,* I silently prayed. We needed this to work.

We unloaded all the stuff we bought at the store on the way down. Many dollars later, we had all her dorm stuff. "Dad might not be too happy," I said to Lauren with a fake smile. Lauren needed bedding, a comforter, toiletries, and a few things to make her dorm fun. I wanted it to be a comfy place for girls to hang out. I also needed to make provisions for Milo. The other students were very helpful; the boys carried the large items, and the girls from Lauren's dorm helped her organize her room. She didn't have a roommate. We thought that would be easier because of Milo.

Lauren and Milo came and spent the night at the hotel with me. We had dinner, watched some TV, and fell asleep. The next morning, we had a nice breakfast in a restaurant that had its music way too loud. Lauren and I giggled about that. Milo enjoyed some bacon.

"He's a funny dog, right, Mom?"

"Yes, he is a funny dog," I said, smiling. We drove to Brooks Academy and met up with her teachers and dorm parent. "I think things are all set," I said. "Lauren, are you okay with me leaving now?" I asked reluctantly.

"Yeah, I'm okay," Lauren said, smiling.

Two girls were playing with Milo. "Hey, Lauren, look at this frog I found," called another student from the pond nearby.

"Okay, bye, Mom." Lauren went running with the girls and Milo. *Huh, that was easier than I expected.* I got in the car and took a deep breath. I was emotionally exhausted, and I still had to drive to St. Louis and fly home.

"Have you talked to Lauren?" My sister Kelly asked me on the phone, about two weeks into Lauren's stay at Brooks.

"Yeah, I try to call her every day. She seems to be doing okay. She had one tiny meltdown, but the staff seemed to do okay at handling it. I happened to be on the phone with her, so I heard the whole thing. She was upset about a comment a boy had made."

"Is she homesick?" Kelly asked.

"I think so. She's also kinda struggling with school. She is just not very strong academically."

"Maybe you should go see her."

"I was thinking about it," I said. "We'll see what the next week brings. I do need to work. I have a job, at least for now." I laughed. "I pray every day that this school will work for her."

"I hope so too," Kelly said. "Time will tell. It's only been two weeks."

Settling back into work was difficult. I had so much on my mind. I was in constant fear that I would get that dreaded phone call. There was a beep on my desk phone, and I heard, "Kari, line three is for you." My stomach did a flip.

"Okay," I said to Nancy, the receptionist. "Hi, this is Kari."

"Hi, Kari. This is Paula at Brooks Academy." My stomach flew into my throat. "Lauren is fine; we do have a little problem, though."

Crap, I thought, *here we go. She's only been there two weeks. What did she do?* Paula explained that Lauren and three other kids took Milo for a walk at a break time from class. *Okay*, I thought, *did something burn down?*

"The students went farther than they should have. They didn't leave campus, but we couldn't find them, and it caused a lot of panic. They are safe now, but we need to uphold the consequences."

I caught myself with a giggle. *She went for a walk too far; no one is hurt, nothing burnt to the ground, and the national guard isn't involved?* I didn't see the problem.

"We have to suspend the students for three days," Paula said.

I choked on my coffee. "What? Are you serious? You can't be serious? Oh man, please don't do this," I pleaded. "Lauren is doing better at Brooks than she has in the last four years of school and you're suspending her for taking a walk. I get consequences, but that is a little harsh." I was panicking.

"Well, that is our rule," Paula stated.

"So what do I do now?"

"Kari?" Nancy interrupted. "Alicia is ready to be roomed, and Layla needs blood drawn."

"Okay, I'll be right there," I said. "So I guess I come get her? I'll have to stay in town then; I'm not flying her home for three days."

"Yes, that would work," Paula said. My head was spinning.

I hung up the phone and started crying. I was tired of the roller coaster. I quickly brushed my tears away, and I pulled Alicia and roomed her and did Layla's blood draw. I bumped into Dr. Dillon.

She knew me well enough that she didn't have to even ask if I was okay. "You'll never guess what happened," I said, and proceeded to tell her the story. "I'm going to have to go down there. I know I've had a lot of time off, but I don't know what else to do. Jared can't go; he's way too busy at work." Dr. Dillon knew what we had been going through, and she'd weathered a lot of the storm with me. My coworkers, on the other hand, had not. *I'm definitely not going to get employee of the month anytime this year*, I thought.

I booked another plane ticket, rented a car, and made reservations at the hotel. I said goodbye to Nikki and Megan. Soon it would be the start of summer vacation. "I'll be back really soon," I said.

"Yep," Megan said. "I'm sure you will." She was fifteen but very bright and wise for her age. She knew what was going on and how all of Lauren's antics over the years has affected me, but she could also see how I was emotionally and physically torn by the effects it was having on her, on Nikki, and on her parents' marriage. That is a lot to understand and wrap your head around at that age.

"When will you be home?" Jared asked.

"I have no idea," I answered. "I need to get Lauren settled after this stupid suspension."

"Hopefully she can handle this okay. We need her to go back to school."

I kissed Jared and left for the airport. I flew to St. Louis, then drove to Carbondale. *More corn and beans,* I thought.

When I arrived to pick up Lauren, I spoke to Paula. "Is there any way that, since Lauren has only been here for ten days, she can go to school and I can pick her and Milo up at three every day, then bring her back each morning?"

She said that would probably work, since she was so new. I nodded my head, and Lauren and I drove off before she could change her mind.

"Mom, I swear I didn't do anything wrong. We went for a stupid walk. Milo needs a walk every day," Lauren said, pleading her case.

"What's done is done, and we move on. You now know not to leave the sight of the teachers," I said sternly.

"Okay, Mom," Lauren said sadly. Milo had his head out the window and his tongue flapping in the wind. Lauren and I giggled. "That funny dog," she said, laughing.

A few days passed. Everything was fine. School was tough for Lauren. She just didn't care about getting an education. On the last day she was to stay with me at the hotel, I told her I was leaving, but in reality, I was staying for a day or two to see how she did.

She wasn't super excited to go back and stay in the dorm. "Can I come home with you?" Lauren said as I dropped her off.

"Lauren, this is a good school, and we need you to go to school here." I tried to be strong, but I was crumbling inside. Lauren was upset but handled it well. She and Milo got out of the car, and I kissed and hugged her goodbye. "I will call you tonight," I said.

"You're going back to St. Louis?" she asked.

"Yes," I lied. "Please be good. I love you."

"Love you too, Mom. Bye."

As I drove away with tears and a gut ache, I thought, *Get through this, Lauren. You can do this. You have to do this.* I took a deep breath.

CHAPTER 5

I TALKED TO MY mom every day; we were very close. She understood Lauren and her antics. She was one of the very few people who had seen Lauren at her worst. She also was one of the few who were able to see Lauren's good and beautiful side. Mom knew what life was like when someone you cared about struggled with mental illness. "Mom, I'll be fine," I pleaded. "Lauren is doing okay. She went back to school in a good mood. I'm going to go to a movie and take it easy, and after the movie I'll go back to the hotel. I'll call you later."

There weren't any movies out that I wanted to see, but I wanted to kill time. I ended up at *The Boss Baby*, a movie that I didn't have to concentrate on. *I'm going to sit here and close my eyes and listen to this very strange movie.* I held my phone, but it was on silent. I felt like it was a bomb and I was just waiting for it to ignite.

About an hour into the movie, the light on my phone turned on. *Shit.* It looked like a text from Lauren. I was truly scared to look at my phone.

"Mom, nobody wants me. I'm going to kill myself."

I got out of my seat and walked out of the theater. The sun was blinding as I tried to get to my car. My eyes tried to adjust to my phone screen. *What the heck is going on?* I thought.

I got a second text from my sister Katie. "Lauren texted me about seeing a text I sent you earlier." I looked at my texts. I called Katie; I needed to figure out what was going on.

"Hello," Katie said in a deep Southern accent. She loves the South and pretends to talk in a deep Southern drawl. Usually, it's quite funny; she is very good at it, and it makes Lauren laugh. I just wasn't in the mood today.

"What the heck is going on?" I asked her.

"I have no idea," she said, in her natural voice. "Lauren said she saw a text from me that I sent you."

"What text?" I asked in a panic. Earlier that day, my sisters and I were discussing some family issues, and one of them was custody of our kids if something were to happen to Jared and me. Katie mentioned that Lauren was hard and she didn't know if she would be the best person to take on that responsibility. To Lauren, it said, *I don't like Lauren. I don't want Lauren.* "For the love of God," I said, frustrated. "I know for a fact she has not seen my phone, and I deleted that text as soon as I read it for this exact reason." I was so mad. *How did she see that text?* I was driving to Brooks Academy. "Katie, I'll call you back." Fuming, irritated, and scared, I pulled into the parking lot of her dorm. I could see Lauren; she was walking out of her dorm.

"Lauren," I said. "What the heck is going on?"

Lauren was crying and very upset. "Mom, I just took all of Milo's medication for his infection."

"His antibiotic?" My throat was tight, and I couldn't swallow. "What? Why? How many? Lauren, why?" I was so confused.

"I saw all the texts from you and Aunt Katie," Lauren said, sniffling.

"How? Where?" I asked.

"I went to study hall when you left, and somehow my computer started getting all your texts."

How is that possible? My head started pounding. *We'll have to figure that out later*, I thought. "Lauren, how many pills did you take?" I tried to act calm. More kids and staff were circling us. Apparently, Lauren had a pretty big meltdown in study hall when she saw the texts, so the students knew something was up. I was sad for her, upset that this happened, and kind of embarrassed that we were doing this in front of students and teachers. "Lauren, let's go. Get Milo." Milo was with another student because Lauren was unable to care for him at that time. He jumped in the backseat.

Lauren didn't know how many pills she'd taken. It vacillated between fifteen and twenty-five. The medication was an anti-fungal for an infection in Milo's lungs. "I need to take you to the ER. I don't have a choice." All of a sudden I was overcome with the realization that it was 7:30 p.m., and the ER was going to be busy. We were going to be there all night. I wanted to start crying, and I had no one to help me.

Lauren was getting more agitated. She cried and talked in circles. "I want to go to meet Jesus. I'm so tired of no one wanting me," she said, sobbing. "I know that I will be happy in heaven. That's what they promise."

"Lauren, I love you so much. The text you saw was out of context. You haven't heard the whole story," I tried to explain.

"Nobody wants me. Do you have any idea what it feels like when nobody likes you, nobody wants to even touch you?" Lauren said.

I had no idea what to say. I wanted nothing more than to scoop her up in my arms and fly away to a tropical island, and forget about all of this. I pulled into the parking lot of the hotel. "Lauren, I need to go into the hotel quick and get stuff, and then we'll go to the ER. I won't be able to leave the ER once we're there." The hospital and the hotel were about a mile from each other. I was concerned about her overdose, but she was healthy, and it was an anti-fungal antibiotic. I thought she'd probably get a stomachache and maybe a headache. I knew it was more important to take her in because of her risk for hurting herself or attempting suicide.

I pulled up to the hotel. Lauren said she and Milo would wait in the car because she didn't want to go inside.

Knowing at this point I couldn't trust her, I rolled the windows down and took the key from the ignition. "Don't go anywhere. I will be right back." There was nothing she could damage in the car, nothing that she could harm herself with. I gathered up our stuff and went to the front desk. I heard sirens close by but didn't give it much thought. I worked in a hospital; I heard sirens every day.

I walked out of the lobby and saw an ambulance. I stopped dead in my tracks. *You have got to be kidding me.* Lauren was sitting on the curb with Milo and crying. I walked over and asked what had happened.

"Is this your daughter?" the paramedic asked.

"Yeah," I said, suddenly getting a headache.

There was a woman standing near Lauren. I looked at her with a confused look. She explained that Lauren had gotten out of the car with Milo and sat on the curb crying. She said she'd happened to be outside and ask Lauren if she was okay, and Lauren told her that she had taken pills and needed to go to the ER. I looked back at the paramedic.

"Ma'am, your daughter told this woman that she took pills and doesn't feel well. Do you know anything about this?" *Seriously? Why is this happening?* I thought, wanting to laugh hysterically at how this was rolling out. I explained the story of how we got there. They said that because they were called, Lauren was a minor, and it was an attempted suicide, they had to take her by ambulance to the ER. I was so mad. I took Milo's leash and walked to my rental car. I got in, started the air, closed the doors, and cried. *How could this get so complicated so quickly?* I screamed into a sweatshirt that was lying in the passenger seat.

I drove slowly to the ER. I figured that they would take a little longer because they needed to do all the assessments and admission paperwork. *This is not going to end well,* I thought. I arrived at the ER and was escorted to Lauren's room. There was a police officer standing outside her room. Apparently, if you're suicidal, you might want to kill others too—at least that was how we were treated. I was speechless. I was sitting in the ER with a folding chair, a suicidal kid, a cop, and a dog. *This can't get any worse,* I kept thinking. I felt trapped, with no one to help me. I was doing this all alone, and all I could do was take a deep breath.

Name? Birthday? Meds, allergies, address? Can you tell me what happened? How many pills? All the normal questions. The one thing missing was compassion. She was being treated like a criminal. I thought to myself again, *Last time I checked, mental health was not a crime.* We saw a doctor, then we sat in that ER for about four hours before someone came in.

"Do you have any idea how much longer?" I asked. "How long do we need to stay here? Nobody has done anything. Usually, with an unknown overdose and an ambulance ride to the ER, I would expect blood work and vital-sign monitoring at the very least. Are you going to monitor her or get an EKG? Lauren was complaining about a racing heartbeat."

The nurse was snippy. "I'll ask the doctor," she said, and left.

"Are you kidding me?" I said. I wanted to laugh. I was losing it, probably from pure exhaustion.

The doctor came in and said that, yes, they should have been doing those things. He wasn't sure why they hadn't been done.

"So what's the plan?" I asked.

"First, she has to be cleared medically. That will take about eight hours. We need to draw labs, wait four hours, and draw again. After she is cleared medically, we then call the psychologist to come in and assess her."

It was eleven thirty, and all I had was a folding chair. I was not pleased. I had nowhere to go and no one here to help me, and I had a dog. I laid my head back against the hard metal chair.

Finally, Lauren was cleared medically. "Do you know how long it will be until we see psych?" I asked the ER doctor.

AWESOME! I THOUGHT. LAUREN was sleeping, as it was three thirty in the morning. Milo was curled up on Lauren's feet at the end of the gurney. The cop was still outside the door. I sat in the folding chair and tried to sleep. *Forget this,* I thought. I asked for a few blankets and made a little bed on the hard tile floor in Lauren's ER room.

I was asleep when the bright light came on in the room. There was a younger man, maybe in his twenties, standing in front of Lauren's bed. We both looked at him with squinted eyes and yawned at the same time. I was trying to focus on what he was doing; I was dazed. He did his assessment, much like the assessment we'd done eight hours ago. I figured she would end up being placed in an inpatient care facility, I just did not know where. This process was taking so long, and now they were having trouble finding an acute facility. Apparently, there was a law in the state if Illinois that minor Medicaid patients were a priority over insured minors in the mental health world. That meant any other kiddos in the ER would get placed before Lauren if they were on Medicaid.

My head was spinning. I was hungry, crabby, and very tired. I was told we had to stay there until they found a placement for her. *Placement?* They wanted her to go to an intense acute adolescent care center. I asked which one, because I was from out of state and my insurance didn't cover every facility. I needed them to be in my network. The young man told me that I couldn't decide where she went and that she had to be transported; I couldn't take her. I imagined lunging out of my metal chair at this person, who really didn't care about us. I was done. I felt like I was going to barf.

I took Milo outside and called Jared. I popped a clonazepam as fast as I possibly could.

When I got back to the room, I sat on the floor of Lauren's room and waited. Lauren was still sleeping. The young man came in and said they'd found a place for her. It was in Terre Haute, Indiana. "What? Where is that?" I asked.

"It's about three hours northeast from here," the young man explained. *Wrong way from Brooks Academy*, I thought. "Here's the paperwork for her admission, and here is the paperwork for her transport. One-way transport costs fifteen hundred dollars, and insurance usually doesn't pay."

"Whatever," I said as I shook my head in total disbelief. It was six in the morning; the transport people were there to pick up Lauren. I couldn't believe that I wasn't allowed to drive her. However, she seemed perfectly okay going with a complete stranger. *Should I be worried or okay with that?* I thought. *Well, it is what it is.* I waited with her, hugged her, and saw her off. I waved, tears streaming down my cheeks, but feeling no emotion. I was overloaded by the incidents and was trying to unscramble and make sense of it all. All I could do was pray. The car rounded the corner and disappeared. She was with a complete stranger, and I had to pay for her to be in this situation. *Deep breath,* I said to myself.

CHAPTER 6

Because Terre Haute, Indiana, was a three-hour drive from Carbondale, Illinois, I had plenty of time to catch up on phone calls. "How are the girls doing?" I asked Jared in a don't-tell-me-if-it's-not-good tone.

"They're doing fine. They just miss you."

"I know. Tell them I'll be home as soon as I can. It shouldn't be too much longer. I think Lauren will be at Terre Haute for less than a week. Then she can go back to Brooks Academy."

I started unloading on Jared. I kept going from super sad to mad to okay to annoyed. *What is wrong with me?* I thought. One minute I was singing "Crash" by New Kids on the Block, and the next minute I wanted to throw the CD out the window. I cried and laughed at the same time. I had very little patience for anyone. I was sure the office was thrilled (not really) that I was still gone.

"Kari, you have a full plate right now. It's normal to feel like this. I'm also having these ups and downs. I know it's frustrating," Jared said. When one of us was drowning, the other had always been there to pull them up. I feared for the day we were both drowning at the same time. "Hang in there, hon, and call me to let me know how she is doing and that you are in Indiana safe and sound."

I still had a little over an hour of my drive, and I was so tired. Lack of sleep was getting to me. When I got tired, I got crabby. I didn't do well on night shifts at the hospital. I drove the rest of the way in silence. I wasn't really sure what I wanted to listen to anyway.

I received a call from Terre Haute; Lauren had arrived and was doing well. They were going to do the admission assessment. Apparently, they had strict visiting hours, and I could only see Lauren once a day, from four to five in the evening. I wanted to see her and make sure she knew I was there in Terre Haute and not abandoning her. I was driving as fast as I could but was still nervous about getting there before five. *Will they let me see her if I'm late?* Butterflies were swirling in my stomach.

I have a love-hate relationship with road construction. Jared is a civil engineer, and his company builds and repairs bridges and roads. But I'm human, which means I hate construction and the confusion it brings. Siri told me to take exit 63. I was driving sixty miles per hour, and the exits came and went so fast. I looked, and exit 63 was blocked off for repairs. Starting to panic, I kept driving. It looked like the other direction was open, so I figured I would just turn around. Then I passed a sign that said it was thirteen miles to the next exit.

"Recalculating," Siri said in a monotone voice. *What?* I didn't have time for that. I started to cry. Oh, and then my gas light flicked on.

I lost it. I cried out loud for no one to hear except Milo. *Why is life so complicated? I'm so mad right now. I'm not home with my husband or kids. I have a dog that needs to run. I need gas, and I need to go to the bathroom. I haven't slept for twenty-four hours, and my child is sitting in a mental institution all by herself.* I screamed. All I could think about was all the kids back home who were going out with friends or a date, laughing and being teenagers. That was something Lauren would never experience.

I was able to get gas and get turned around. I stopped crying. I looked at my phone and kept going in the direction Siri was pointing me. I passed restaurants and stores, malls and houses, looking for the facility. I turned into a long driveway. "This must be it," I told Milo. Milo picked his head up and looked at me. "Let's go, boy. Let's see if we can find Lauren." He started breathing harder and wagging his tail. "You're a funny dog," I said to him.

This facility was brand new. They were still doing construction on parts of it. I walked up to the door, but it was locked. I rang the bell. I heard a click, and it let me open the door. I walked in. There was a new-construction smell. The room was white but decorated nicely. There was a child who looked to be about ten crying and leaning on his mother. I guess he was there for a self/parent admission. I stood in line and waited.

"Next," called the woman behind tempered glass.

I was nervous. "Um, hi. I'm Kari, Lauren's mom."

"Hi, Kari. Please sign here and here."

I was a little worried. I was used to our hometown hospital—yes, they annoyed me, but at least it was a familiar system. I held on to Milo tightly. He wanted to sniff and explore. I didn't want the staff to get annoyed and say he needed to leave. I didn't know what I would do with him. It was really hot, and he couldn't stay in the car.

I hadn't missed visiting time. I was so relieved. I was escorted to an office with a table and chairs and a desk with a computer.

There was a large window looking out to dirt and more construction. *When this is finished, it will be a great view of the courtyard,* I thought.

Lauren was waiting for me in the office. "Hi, Lauren," I said, and gave her a big hug.

"Hi, Milo," Lauren said excitedly. Milo was wagging his tail, very happy to see Lauren.

A woman walked into the room. She was about thirty, pretty, and nicely dressed. "Hi, Kari?" she asked, holding out her hand.

"Hi," I said, and shook her hand.

"Lauren and I have met," she said, smiling at Lauren. "She seems nice."

I was not in the happy visiting mood. I was tired, but I smiled anyway.

"Here are just a few papers we need to sign. Medications, a release of information, and contact people with phone numbers. Will you be staying in Terre Haute?"

"Uh . . . yeah." I stumbled over my words. "I don't know where I'm going to stay."

"Okay, well just let us know when you find out." She continued to smile.

"Okay," I said, not smiling. We finished up with the paperwork and walked to the cafeteria.

There were picnic-style tables lined up. The room was big and open, with lots of windows and light. Visiting families sat with their children, one patient per table. Lauren sat at a table by the window. I joined her; Milo laid down on the tile floor under the table.

"Was your ride okay?" I asked her.

"Yeah, I slept the whole way. I was really tired."

You don't say, I thought. I forced a smile.

"I'm sorry, Mom."

"I know, Lauren." We had one hour to visit, play a game, and have a juice box. "We don't get to see the unit?" I asked confused.

"No, they only let parents go to that door," Lauren said, pointing to the first set of doors. There were two glass doors that were locked, another set of locked glass doors about fifty feet farther. The hallways were sterile, all tile with white walls.

"Are you going to be okay? Are they nice?" I was concerned. All the staff wore gray scrubs and had walkie-talkies. *Well, now I know how prison feels,* I thought as I tried to keep myself from getting sick.

Lauren looked sad. I wished she didn't have to be here, now. I started crying again.

"Mom, I'll be fine."

"Listen, Lauren: you need to behave. These people look like they mean business." I didn't want to leave her here, but I didn't have a choice. I was trying to guide her, as I was terrified for her. Wiping my tears, I said goodbye. I watched as the kids were escorted through the glass doors until I couldn't see Lauren anymore.

I slowly walked to the car. I was emotionally and physically drained. I slumped down in the car and drove out the long driveway. *Bye, Lauren,* I thought. *Please be good.* I looked at Milo, took a deep breath, and went to look for a hotel.

CHAPTER 7

Driving down the main road, I stopped at a large, well-known hotel. I pulled up to the door and got out. "Stay here, Milo. I'll be back in two minutes," I said. Milo looked at me in a total panic, like I was selling the car with him in it. I walked into the lobby and up to the desk. I overheard the lady tell another couple that they were full. Apparently, there was something happening in town; all the hotels were full. *You have got to be kidding me; of course they are all full.* I was going to be sick now.

I was next in line. "Hi, do you have a room, please?" I wasn't sure why I was asking. I knew the answer. The lady working behind the desk looked at me and gave me the same answer she'd given the couple ahead of me. She was very kind and called around to a few other hotels, but they were all full too. I sat on the fireplace hearth in the lobby, called Jared, and cried. I literally could not make decisions at this point. To top it off, it was pouring rain.

I got up and started walking out the automatic glass sliding doors. "Miss? Miss? Excuse me, miss?" I turned around. The lady from the desk was standing in front of me. "I'm sorry, I overheard some of your conversation and, well . . . we do keep a room or two for emergencies." She looked at me and said, "Well, I think this might be an emergency."

I looked at her in disbelief. "Seriously? Oh my gosh, I'm so thankful. My daughter is in the hospital, and I drove with a dog all the way here, it's raining, and"—I started to cry again—"I didn't sleep at all last night." I was rambling.

She smiled. "It's okay, dear. Let's get you into a room. I have one on the first floor. It's near the back exit so you can take your dog out easily."

I told her I had never been so grateful. "Thank you, God, for looking over me," I whispered. We walked to the room, and she helped me with all my stuff. "You have no idea how much I appreciate this." It may have seemed like a small thing, but for me, it meant the world.

She nodded and said, "My pleasure."

I called Jared right away and let him know I was in a room and going to sleep. I told him all about the kind lady at the desk. Jared later said he called the front desk and personally thanked her. There were still people out there, people who wanted to be kind. That made me smile.

The next few days were very long. Milo and I drove around, took naps, and went to a nice dog park located right on a river. At four o'clock I would go to the facility, sign my name, walk to the cafeteria, visit for an hour, and then watch Lauren walk back through the glass doors. The doors that led to who-knows-where.

"How's it going?" I asked.

Lauren started telling me about kids who got "booty-juiced"— an injection that they gave to the kids, usually in their butts, hence the name. It was a sedative for unruly patients. "Mom, the kids are not friendly here. They get into fights with each other. I want to come with you. I miss you."

"I miss you too, Lauren. All you need to do is get through this."

"Do I get to go back to Brooks Academy?"

"I hope so," I said with a sigh. "So let's make this work."

She smiled.

I'd been in Indiana for four days, and I wanted to go home. I drove, mesmerized by the light as the sun was setting. I at least wanted to be doing something with Lauren that didn't involve a hospital. I called the other girls at home. Megan was at cheer practice, and Nikki was watching TV. "What are you watching, Nikki?" I asked, wondering what to talk about. It had been about two weeks since I was last home.

"Oh, nothing, just a kids' show," Nikki responded, sounding preoccupied. "Mommy, when are you coming home?"

"Soon, I hope. Lauren seems to be doing well. I'm hoping she gets discharged tomorrow." I was torn between wanting to be with Lauren and wanting to be home with Jared and the kids. I walked into the hotel room and collapsed on the bed, not really from physical exhaustion but from emotional exhaustion. I must have slept well, because I woke up in the same position I went to sleep in.

Later that day, the facility called and said they were discharging Lauren. I had quite the stash to pack up: groceries, dog food, suitcases, bowls, toiletries, and my pillow. I held on to Milo's leash and tried to gather as much as I could in one trip. I got it done in about three trips, Milo with me every time.

On my way to pick up Lauren, I called Paula at Brooks Academy. I was excited to tell her that Lauren was cleared to come back. "Hi, Paula, how are you?" I said. "I just wanted to tell you that Lauren is getting to leave Terre Haute today and I will be able to bring her back." Lauren was doing reasonably well, and she needed to be in school—this school.

"Oh, I'm glad she's doing better," Paula said in an everyday tone. I was getting a bad feeling. "Kari, I spoke to admissions, and we feel that Lauren is not ready to come back to Brooks Academy. We feel she needs more therapy."

I stopped breathing; my world was spinning once again. "Why? Where?" I said with a trembling voice. "We fought so hard for the district to pay for this. Why is this happening? I just moved her in. She's going to be crushed. She was so excited to come back. She even has a prom dress. She was excited to see her friends."

Paula sighed. "I'm sorry, but we feel it's for the best. After she gets adequate therapy and is not suicidal, she is welcome back."

"Okay, thank you." I hung up and started crying. How could they do this to her? Could we not catch a break? I called Jared and explained the situation.

"What should we do?" Jared said. "Another treatment center? I don't know, maybe Aspen?"

Aspen was a wilderness therapy program. Lauren had gone there about a year prior and seemed to do well. It was outside, twenty-four-seven. The kids ate, slept, bathed, went to the bathroom, showered, had therapy, hiked, biked, and rock-climbed for twelve weeks—all outside. I thought that would buy time and fulfill the requirement for her to go back to Brooks Academy.

I dialed the Aspen number. "Hi, my name is Kari. My daughter Lauren was a resident about a year ago. We were wondering if she could come and do the program or part of it again, like a reboot?"

"Yes, that would be fine," said the woman on the phone.

"When could she start?" I asked.

"As soon as you get the paperwork to us."

"Okay. We're currently in Terre Haute, Indiana."

"Great. Get us the paperwork, and we'll see you in a few days."

I hung up feeling a little better. The district was paying for Brooks Academy; maybe they would pay for Aspen too. I called Jared and explained the situation. "On our way to Salt Lake, we can talk to Krystal at the school district and see if there's something they can do."

"It's not an academic setting, so they probably won't fund it," he tried to explain to me.

I pondered what he said. "I'll reach out to Krystal and we'll go from there. I'm at the hospital to pick up Lauren. Will you call your mom and dad and ask them to watch the girls and then meet us in St. Louis?" I was out of breath.

Jared sighed. "Okay, I'll be in touch." I could see him rolling his eyes.

I was reluctant to tell Lauren; I didn't want a meltdown when we had a three-hour drive to St. Louis and then another eighteen to Salt Lake. Milo and I arrived at the hospital. It was cooler, so I was able to leave Milo in the car with the windows down for the few minutes I was inside. Lauren seemed happier now then she was when I'd met her in the office a few days ago. The same well-dressed woman was there to say goodbye.

"You don't have to tell me twice!" Lauren exclaimed, and she was out the door.

I gathered her items and looked down the long sterile hallway at the glass doors. I got the chills.

I started driving. After a few minutes, Lauren noticed I wasn't driving south to Carbondale. "Where are we going?" she asked.

I didn't want to answer, so I held my breath. "We're going to spend the night in St. Louis." She nodded. I was putting off telling Lauren for as long as I could.

A few hours into the drive, Lauren asked, "Mom, are you going to stay at Brooks for a few days or are you going to go home?"

My stomach did a flip. The palms of my hands started to feel clammy. "Well, Lauren . . ." I didn't know how to start. "I was able to speak to Brooks Academy, and Paula said that they would like you to have more professional help. She did say that, if you wanted, you could go back there after you finish."

Lauren looked at me. No yelling, no crying, just a blank stare. "Of course she did." She looked out the window. This poor kid couldn't catch a break. The rain had started, and it dripped slowly onto the car windshield. Milo was asleep in the back. There was no music on; it was quiet except for the *swish, swish* of the wipers on the front window.

I could see that Lauren was really upset. She looked so defeated. Yelling was hard to deal with, but complete silence with no emotion was torture. *Why is there no one to help us with this? Why am I fighting this battle alone? I don't know what I'm doing,* I thought. *Public schools are supposed to provide a free and appropriate education to every child. There have to be other kids with moderate to severe behaviors that get adequate help, but where are they?* I had a headache. I looked in the passenger seat. "Lauren, are you okay?"

She remained silent and continued staring out the window.

CHAPTER 8

THE DRIVE SEEMED VERY long. We drove through St. Louis to a smaller town called O'Fallon, where my aunt and uncle lived. Aunt Char, Uncle Melvin, and their three boys had vacationed with my family for over twenty years. I had many fond memories from the lake resort we stayed at. Char and Melvin now lived on a small lake just west of St. Louis. We turned onto their main road and then onto a dirt road. Then another dirt road took us to their driveway. I felt very "far, far into the woods," as my mom would say. The driveway was paved and circled the house. There was a fire pit off in the distance and a basketball hoop near the asphalt driveway. Melvin loved to collect things, and he always knew what was needed and where to get it. Char loved gardening, and there was a garden with vegetables and big and colorful flowers. The lake was peeking through the groves of trees. The water looked refreshing. There was a dock, and a boat bobbed gently back and forth on the water. There was a tire swing tied to a tree near the water, which swayed in the wind. Melvin and Char were sitting on the front porch, which wrapped around the side and back of the house. I waved.

Milo was ready to get out and play. He knew we were someplace fun when Melvin and Char's two golden retrievers came running up to the car. I opened the car door, and Milo leaped onto the asphalt driveway. He started sniffing and marking his territory.

Lauren was still quiet, and I was getting more worried. The outdoors was therapeutic for Lauren. She seemed to need the sun and the fresh air to exist. Summer or winter, she could take what Mother Nature dished out. "I'll watch Milo, Mom," Lauren said quietly as she got out of the car. I watched her walk slowly and peacefully to the lake, following her dog.

I watched her down by the lake—no friends, no parties, no extracurricular sports. *No freedom,* I thought. I walked heavily to the back of the car to unload the small amount of stuff we had and then turned and walked back to the house. I didn't feel like socializing, but I needed to try. Jared would be here tomorrow, and then we'd take off for Salt Lake. I visited for a bit, then went inside to unpack. Milo had followed me in. He sniffed a little and, within a minute of being inside, he raised his leg and peed near the TV. I was mortified. *Seriously, Milo? Really? Here?* He hadn't had an accident in a long time. I got a paper towel and wiped it up. "I'm so sorry," I said to Char and Melvin, not having a clue what else I could say.

I crawled into bed that night. Lauren and I were in the same room but separate beds. With tears in my eyes, looking over at Lauren sleeping, I drifted to sleep.

I WAS STARTLED AWAKE by my phone ringing. *I need to turn that down. That ring is super annoying,* I thought. "Hi, Mom," I answered, dazed. "How are you?" I said, wishing she was here. My mom was the quintessential grandma. She was caring, loved to give hugs, and could have a conversation with anyone. She was a people person, and still talked to her high school and college friends weekly. She kept in touch with every neighbor and friend from the various places we lived. If someone were sick or had surgery, Mom would be there with a peach pie. Just thinking about that made me hungry.

Mom loved Lauren so much, and it killed me to have to tell her this. "Mom, we are driving to Salt Lake. Lauren is going to Wilderness again. Brooks Academy feels she needs more professional help. They said she could go back there when she completes the therapy." I closed my eyes, not sure if I would get Lecturing Mom or Sobbing Mom.

She started crying. Growing up in the fifties in a small town in the Midwest, mental health had been a very taboo topic for her. Everything was swept under the rug, and all families were supposed to appear perfect. My grandmother struggled with depression, and maybe some other issues, but no one knew because people didn't talk about it. My grandfather was a hardworking salesman. He traveled all week, while my grandma stayed home with four kids under the age of five. Mom was very sensitive when it came to mental health. She had seen her mother struggle, and now she was watching her oldest granddaughter do the same.

"I'm sorry, Mom. It'll be okay. Lauren is getting used to the idea of Wilderness. At least it's not a hospital setting. She loves the outdoors. I'll talk to you soon." I pushed the "end" button on my phone, sat up, and looked outside.

Lately, I had noticed myself struggling with socializing. It was just too much work. I knew I was overwhelmed and stressed, but didn't know how to get past that. I'd had about five different nursing jobs since I got my license twenty years ago, and I was not in contact with any of my old coworkers. I didn't keep in touch with old neighbors or friends. I would maybe send a Christmas card—maybe.

In the last few years, everything had started getting more difficult. When people saw Lauren struggling, I knew they felt bad, but they walked away. By the time Lauren was in about fourth grade, the phone had stopped ringing. No invitations to birthday parties or playdates. Good friends stopped inviting us over as a family. I felt empty. I figured people just didn't want to be around mental health issues. Maybe they didn't know what to do. Maybe they felt that their kids would pick up on bad habits, or that it was contagious and they too would become bipolar or severely depressed.

I went out into the kitchen and poured myself a cup of coffee. Lauren was already outside running with Milo. Lauren had a stick and was playing fetch with the dog, although I was not quite sure who was doing the fetching. The grass was still wet with morning dew. *Hopefully his paws won't be muddy,* I thought. I sat at the kitchen table and talked with Melvin and Char. They had a big picture window in their kitchen, so I could watch Lauren and just relax.

"I think Jared is planning on arriving around eleven. I'm going to take a shower and get organized," I said as I put my cup in the sink.

"I'll keep an eye on Lauren," said Melvin with a wink.

"Thanks, Melvin," I said with a smile. Lauren couldn't be left alone. Like a toddler, she found things that no one else could find if they tried, got into messes that no one else knew were possible, and talked to anyone about anything. Sometimes strangers took offense to that. I was always on my toes.

"Jared called and said he would be here in a few minutes. There is a lot of traffic on the interstate," Char said as she cleaned up breakfast dishes. "It may take him a little longer." Lauren was sitting on the tire swing, slowly swaying back and forth. She looked as if she were in deep thought. I was going to miss her so much, but I was so happy she was willing to go to Wilderness again. She did well there. Then she could go back to Brooks Academy; that was the goal.

"Dad's here!" Lauren yelled as Jared drove up the driveway. Milo was in a full sprint across the lawn to get to Jared. It was a beautiful day, and the sky was bright blue, much better than that rain the other day.

"Lauren, let's get everything loaded up in the van," I called to her. She had run down to the lake. "Lauren, don't get wet or muddy. I only have one pair of shoes for you!" I yelled again.

"Mom, can we get crafts to do in the car?" she yelled back.

I wasn't about to continue yelling back and forth to have a conversation. When I didn't answer, Lauren ran back up from the lake.

"Mom, can we?" Lauren said, out of breath.

"Why are you muddy?" I asked as I looked at her dirty knees, hands, and feet.

"I caught a frog, but I let him go," she said casually.

"Lauren, I can't drive to a craft store right now." I was hoping this didn't end up in an argument. "We have movies and books, and you have your iPod."

She looked at me, frustrated, and rolled her eyes.

"Go over to the hose and try to wash off the mud. I'll get you an old towel," I said as I walked inside to double-check that we didn't forget anything. When I came out with the towel, Milo ran up to me soaking wet. "Lauren, why is Milo wet?"

"Because I bathed him. He wanted a bath," Lauren explained to me.

"In the lake? Seriously?" I could see Char and Melvin chuckle. "Now he's wet, and you're drenched." I went to the van and sorted through her clothes. "Here, Lauren, go dry off with this towel and put this on," I said as calmly as I could. I could see Jared talking to Melvin, both working hard to hide their smirks. "With Lauren, every day is an adventure," I said. Lauren came bounding out the door.

"Bye, Char and Melvin! Thanks for everything," she said happily.

"We'll be in touch," I said as I hugged them goodbye. "Thank you for everything."

Lauren and Milo sat in the backseat. Milo smelled like a wet dog and Lauren was digging in the snack bag. "I'm starving. Can we stop and eat?" she asked.

I looked at Jared. I was already tired, and it was only noon. I plugged Salt Lake City into my phone—nineteen hours to go.

Lauren had found some Skittles and settled in to watch a movie. Milo was sleeping, and Jared put on a new album from New Kids on the Block. He knew that was one thing that would make me smile. I put my head back and looked out the window at the corn and beans and beans and corn. I looked at Lauren and couldn't help but think about her life. All the things we had tried over the years. *How exactly did we get here?* I was exhausted. I closed my eyes and drifted to sleep.

CHAPTER 9

2001

"SARAH IS IN ROOM one, and Ellen is in room two," I said as I looked down and walked quickly past her door. I was already exhausted from the morning at home. Lauren was at a new daycare, so I was extra uneasy today. Dr. Dillon walked into the clinic half an hour late from a delivery. This was pretty typical, as babies don't always plan the most convenient time to be born.

"How did it go?" I asked.

Dr. Dillon looked at me and smiled. "They're so happy. It was a girl, and the delivery went great." She paused and looked at her schedule for the day. "So what do we have?" Dillon asked, walking toward the room.

"Sarah is in room one. She's twenty-four weeks and feeling crampy. Ellen C. is in room two; she's here for her postpartum checkup." I handed Dr. Dillon the chart.

We kept the rooms full of patients so that they weren't just sitting in the waiting room. We did our best. Sometimes patients need a little extra TLC, and Dr. Dillon was good at spending that extra minute or two with her patients. Today was going to be busy. I looked at the schedule, and with a deep breath I mumbled, "Sixteen patients." I was trying to keep a positive attitude, but I was so tired.

Startling me out of my daze, I heard, "Kari?"

"Yeah?" I said, feeling a little on edge.

"There's a call on line three for you."

"Okay," I said with a sinking feeling in my stomach, and picked up the phone. "Hello," I said.

"Kari, this is Dianne." I could hear Lauren crying in the background. Lauren was about nine months old now and hated to be away from me, ever. "Lauren is really upset and has been crying since you dropped her off."

I felt nauseated. "Okay, did you try a bottle?"

"Yep."

"How about a pacifier or her favorite bear?"

"Yep," she answered, annoyed.

Just then, Dr. Dillon came out of room one and gave me a piece of paper with labs and instructions on it. "Sarah is waiting for you when you're off the phone," she said. I could tell she was wondering why I was upset and on the phone. She walked into room two.

"Umm, Dianne, I have a patient I need to tend to. Can you call me in half an hour if she is still crying?" I hung up the phone. I was starting to panic. *Focus*, I thought.

The office had four doctors, each doctor had an RN, and everyone had a full schedule. I went in and gave Sarah instructions and sent her to the lab for blood work. I quickly cleaned the room to get it ready for the next patient.

"Kari, do you have time to give an injection?" another nurse asked.

"Ah, yeah, gimme a sec." I felt myself getting more anxious. I roomed the next patient, got vitals, and gave her a gown to put on. "Dr. Dillon will be in soon," I said to the patient.

I grabbed the injection sheet and prepared the syringe. I started to give the shot only to hear, "Kari, you have a call on line four."

"Hold on. I'll be there in a minute." I finished the injection and sent the patient on her way. "Hello," I answered timidly.

"Hi, Kari, this is Dianne. Lauren is screaming, and she is starting to make the other kids upset. I don't know what to do with her." Dianne was starting to sound frustrated, and that scared me.

"Okay, Dianne, I can come get her, but I need to find someone to fill in for me."

"Okay, well, hurry up."

Just then Dr. Dillon came out of room two. "Ellen needs to schedule a procedure. Find a date, then let her know. We need to have the date coincide with her cycle *blah blah blah blah*." I didn't hear anything. I started to cry.

Dr. Dillon looked at me funny. "What's wrong, Kari?"

I told her what had happened and that I needed to get Lauren. Dr. Dillon was a mother and a wife. She had a very busy household, so she understood why I was so upset. "Okay, I'll let the nurse manager know. We'll see if we can get someone down here to take over for you. In the meantime, could you get Ellen set up for surgery and get the next patient roomed?"

I was cleaning the room when the phone rang again and I heard my name. "I'll pick it up. What line?"

"Line two," the receptionist said.

Dianne sounded pissed. "Kari, you need to get this kid, and she is not welcome back. Find another daycare."

"Okay, Dianne, I'm getting out of here as fast as I can."

She hung up the phone. I was in total panic mode now. I was shaking and couldn't think straight.

"Kari?"

"Yeah." I was quickly losing my cool.

"Sam Morten is on line three; she said her water broke."

I looked at Dr. Dillon. She said calmly, "Have her go to the hospital. I'll call in orders." Dillon walked into her office and called the hospital to give orders. I felt like such a failure.

I needed to call somebody to get Lauren. Jared was out of town for work. My parents were in Pennsylvania, and Jared's parents were out of town too. I was worried Dianne would hurt her. She sounded awfully mad. I tried some friends, but nobody was home. I called my neighbor Jan, hoping she would answer even though she worked last night. The phone rang four times, and finally, Jan said hello with a scratchy voice.

"Hi, Jan, this is Kari. Lauren is at this new daycare . . ." I continued to tell her the details. When I hung up the phone, Dr. Dillon was at my desk.

"What's the plan?" she asked.

"My neighbor is going to get Lauren. I still need to leave, though. Jan worked last night and works tonight again, and she needs to sleep."

After about an hour, I found another nurse to cover for me. I was a mess. *What happened to Lauren to make her cry like that? Is she hurt?* I drove to Jan's house. I was on the phone with my mom, and we were both crying. I didn't know what I was going to do. I had to work the next day and didn't know where was I going to send Lauren.

When I walked into Jan's, I saw Lauren sleeping on her lap. "What happened?" I said.

"Nothing," Jan said. "I went to get Lauren, and she came right to me and stopped crying. She was really upset, though."

I could see the ringlets on her head, wet from sweat. Her little eyes were red and swollen, and she was breathing small, quick breaths. She opened her eyes. "Mama," she said, and started crying again.

"Hi, Lauren. Should we go home?" I picked her up from Jan's lap. She was drenched with sweat. She put her face on my shirt. *What did she do to you?* I thought. "I will forever be grateful for your help today," I said to Jan. "Thank you." I gave her a big hug.

Jan smiled. "Not a problem." She loved little Lauren too.

Lauren smiled at me, and we walked to the car.

CHAPTER 10

I WALKED IN THE door and set Lauren down on the kitchen floor with her toys. Bailey, our Sheltie, came over and gave her kisses. "Hi, Bailey—good dog," I said.

"Baybay," Lauren said, trying to copy me.

I walked to the fridge and got out a yogurt. I sat down next to Lauren and started feeding her. "Yum, banana," I said to her.

"Nana, mmm," Lauren said back to me. We laughed. She rubbed her mouth and then her hair, making them sticky.

"How can anybody not love you to pieces?" I said to her.

"Mama," she said, and rubbed her eyes.

"Are you tired?" I wiped her hands and face and tried my best with her hair. It was fine, soft, and blonde. I walked her to her room and laid her down in her crib.

She looked at her favorite stuffed bear, which had rainbow colors all over. "Barbar," she said, smiling.

"Okay, you go night-night. Mommy is right here." I tiptoed out of the room.

Lauren must be really tired from today. She never goes down that easily, I thought. I sat down at the kitchen table and looked at the list of daycares that I had called previously. The only one I would send her to after today was Debi's. Debi was a neighbor who had an in-home daycare. She was terrific and had excellent references, but she had said that her daycare was full and that she wanted to downsize. Nervously, I dialed her number.

"Hi, Debi. It's Kari. Is this a bad time?" I asked.

"Actually, it is a good time. All the kiddos are taking naps," she said.

I told Debi of the horrible experience I'd had earlier. I told her that Jan had gone over and picked Lauren up. She felt awful about what happened. I asked her about taking Lauren. "I'm desperate," I said. "I don't know where to go, and I know you would take good care of Lauren." I took a deep breath. Jared was out of town from Monday to Friday. I knew it was part of his job, but I missed him and his help. *You can't bring the road home to fix. You have to go to the road,* Jared would tell me. That seemed pretty basic, but I hated it all the same. I offered to pay Debi more per day for Lauren. I think she knew she might have some rougher days.

Debi took a deep breath. "Can I think it over a bit? I want to talk to other moms and get a feel for everyone's plans—whether they're staying, leaving, or maybe expecting."

"Of course," I said. I needed an answer, but I also needed to respect Debi's space and her decision. I hung up the phone, sat down on the couch, and closed my eyes. *What a day,* I thought.

By four thirty, I still had not heard from Debi, and I needed to call the office. I got Dr. Dillon's voice mail. "Hey, Dr. Dillon, it's Kari. I am still trying to nail down a daycare provider. I have one in mind, but I'm waiting for her final approval. I don't think I can work tomorrow. I'm really sorry. Call me back, bye." I hated to leave a message, but I wanted her to hear it before the clinic closed so that they could find someone to fill in. I started doing laps in my kitchen. Lauren was now awake and was utterly mesmerized by the Baby Mozart video playing on the VCR. I waited and waited.

When five o'clock came, I figured I wouldn't hear from her that evening. Lauren and I ate dinner, bathed, put on super soft pj's, and went to bed. Since Jared had been out of town, Lauren had become my snuggle bug. I couldn't get her to sleep in her own bed at night, but I figured this phase would pass. If Lauren was sleeping with me, she slept all night. In her bed, she was up multiple times at night, crying and crying. She couldn't seem to calm down by herself, but she could with my help. I'd missed many hours of precious sleep, and on many mornings I would leave for work in tears because I was so tired.

I was in bed reading when the phone rang. I answered the phone and crossed my fingers. "Hi, Debi," I said, and held my breath.

"So I think it would work if Lauren wanted to come play with us." I was so amazed and grateful. "Lauren could start tomorrow." *This will make everything easier*, I thought. I hung up the phone. I felt relieved. I reached over and rubbed Lauren's back for a moment as I closed my eyes.

Friday night finally arrived, and Jared was coming home. "I made your favorite dinner," I said, smiling. He always came home a mess from being out in the hot sun working in construction, sweating and moving things in the dirt. When he first walked in the door, Lauren would eye him up and down, trying to figure out who he was. After his shower, she would toddle toward him, shouting, "Dada!" The weekends came and went. Lauren and I would wave to Daddy as he drove away in his red pickup.

"Lauren, let's go to Debadeb's and play." Lauren, almost one year old, came to me on her hands and knees. *Almost walking*, I thought. Lauren started calling Debi "Debadeb" the first week. She was doing well at daycare, with the occasional crying spell. There were other kids to play with, and Debi had a great big backyard.

Debi was good at filling me in on the days' happenings. "She always stops crying when we go outside," Debi said. "The kid loves playing outside."

I smiled and picked up my happy, sand-covered baby girl.

It was September, and Lauren's birthday was in a few weeks. I was tired and moody. Nothing sounded good. *What is going on?* I thought. A thought suddenly popped into my head. *No*, I thought. *No way.* I had a pregnancy test in the house. *Do I dare try?*

I got ready for work and dressed and fed Lauren. I went back into the bathroom and looked at the test. I started laughing and then crying. Jared was out of town and I couldn't reach him, so I called my mom. "Hey," I said, crying, "What are you doing June 14?"

"What's wrong?" she asked. "Is Lauren okay?" She was in a panic.

"Well . . ." I paused. "Lauren is going to be a big sister." Mom was so excited. "Okay, I need to drop Lauren off and get to work," I said.

"Here's Lauren's bag and her bear," I said to Debi. "I will be back soon, Lauren. Bye-bye." I waved, and she crawled to the toys. "So, Debi"—I was sweating even thinking about asking her—"would you by any chance have room in nine months for another baby?" Deb smiled. I felt like I was pressing my luck, but I was just as surprised as she was.

"Of course," she said with a huge smile.

It was almost eight o'clock, and I was running late. The morning radio DJ said, "Someone said there was an explosion in New York in one of the World Trade Centers." I had never been to New York, so this didn't mean much to me, but I felt sad; there were people hurt, maybe even killed. I parked my car and walked into the clinic. People were buzzing all over.

"What's going on?" I asked. I walked into the break room just as a plane flew into the second tower. Everyone was confused, even the reporters.

"Did you see that plane?" a coworker asked. "It looked like a regular passenger plane."

People started screaming. I looked back at the TV screen to see the second tower crumbling to the ground. Then the first tower started to fall. We all stood there and watched. I didn't know what to feel.

I called my dad, who worked at the Pittsburgh airport. "Dad, what is going on?"

"Two planes hit the World Trade Center, and I just heard another plane crashed not far from here. I need to go; they're evacuating the airport."

I heard a coworker from the first floor yell, "The Pentagon was hit!"

I looked at the TV. "We're under attack," the broadcasters said. I walked to my desk. A tear came down my cheek. I rubbed my tummy. *You are safe, little one, my little miracle baby,* I thought. *For so many reasons, I will never forget this day.*

Sad weeks passed, mourning for all those who lost loved ones. There seemed to be so many people who knew someone who had a family member that was killed in the towers. *We are so frail as humans,* I thought, *We're like a speck of sand floating in the universe.*

Lauren's birthday was right around the corner. We planned a little party with grandparents, family, and friends. Lauren's little friend Page, who was about six months old, and little cousin Madison, who was fourteen months, were able to come. Lauren took her firsts steps the day before her birthday.

"Happy birthday to Lauren," we all sang. "Happy birthday to you." She was elbow deep in cake and frosting. We told everyone we were expecting and about how I found out on 9-11. "I'm still so shaken up by the news about what happened with the World Trade Centers," I said in disbelief.

Mom let a moment pass and then said, "I can't believe Lauren is one year old today. I feel like this new baby just came home from the hospital."

I laughed. "We didn't know what we were doing or what becoming parents really meant."

CHAPTER 11

"Lauren," I hollered towards the next room. "Do you have your shoes on?"

No answer.

"Lauren Grace, where are you?" I picked up Megan, who was now six months old, and sat her on the ground to play. I walked into the bathroom. Evidently, I'd left the two inches of water in the tub after bathing Megan. Lauren did in fact have her shoes on, along with a cute little outfit. Yet there she sat in the bathtub, soaking wet. "Honey, you already had your bath," I said as I giggled. I laughed and couldn't help but run and get my camera. Lauren had huge dimples, and her laugh lit up the room. Her hair was blond, and a barrette held a small piece of hair up. Her eyes were big, round, chocolate-chip cookies. *I could get lost in those eyes*, I thought.

She was a very bright little girl and loved learning new things. She was so inquisitive; she would stare at something, not just to look at it but to figure out how it worked. Lauren was doing all the things a little girl should be doing, but I was starting to see something was off. Her mood was just a little bit different than other kids'. She was fine and happy most of the time. But when she was mad, having a tantrum, we started to see the difference. Other kids calmed down, but Lauren couldn't. If she were sent to time-out or had something taken away, we would be looking at a 1–2 hour meltdown.

Lauren was about five years old, and she and Megan were playing. I wanted to comb her hair, which she hated, but I was tired of having to deal with meltdowns because of stupid little things. "Lauren, let's get ready and we can go outside." Lauren loved going outside—in rain, heat, snow, or ice.

"No, I don't want my hair brushed," Lauren said.

"Lauren, we need to brush it. Here, you do it."

"Nope, not gonna brush my hair."

"Okay, fine. Whatever," I said, frustrated. I had to pick my battles. "I need you to brush your teeth now then."

"No, I don't want to," she said, starting to whine.

"Lauren, here is your toothbrush. Either you brush them, or I will."

Oh, it was on. Lauren stood her ground.

I yelled at her. I was so frustrated. I went outside and called my friend. "How hard is it to do basic hygiene?" I said. "I'm not even asking her to do it on her own. When I tell her to do something, I swear she does the opposite just to spite me. If I told her to jump out of a burning house, she would sit down just to prove she didn't have to."

When I felt better, I came back in the house. "Lauren, where are you?" I said. I walked into the family room and saw Lauren hiding under the table. I was confused. "Lauren, let's make lunch."

She didn't say anything.

"Lauren, will you come out and help me?"

Nothing. I was getting a little concerned now. I walked up to her, and she cowered like an injured animal. I had never seen her like this. I tried other things to get her to come out. I finally got the cordless phone and sat in the chair. We had started working with a child therapist, so I gave her a call and explained what was going on. I tried a few different tactics to no avail.

The counselor said, "Go sit in the middle of the room. Don't talk, don't make eye contact. Just sit and wait until she comes to you."

That seems strange, I thought, but did what she said. I sat and sat and sat. After about thirty minutes, Lauren started to move closer, closer, closer until she was about a foot from me. I didn't move. She put her hand out to touch me like I was an animal she wasn't sure wouldn't bite. She laid her little hand on my leg. I stayed still. She put her other hand on my leg. Slowly, she crawled into my lap. We sat there for a long time, not saying anything. I held her, wishing I could keep her safe in a bubble forever. I knew this world was going to be less than forgiving. I started to cry.

An hour later, Lauren was a happy little girl, playing normal little-girl games. She cycled from happy to mad to sad to happy multiple times per day. My guard was always up.

Lauren was the neighborhood social butterfly. She knew everyone's name, and she was articulate and seemed to handle herself well with adults. Everyone loved her—except kids her age. Other kids were starting to go to birthday parties, or I would see them out at a movie with another little friend. Lauren was going to turn six, so I thought we could have a little party. I wanted to see how she interacted with her peers, so I invited the girls from her class. There were about fourteen girls. I planned on a few different games and then cake and ice cream. It was pretty low-key. I was so hoping this would let the other girls know that Lauren liked parties and would love a friend.

We started by playing pin the tail on the donkey. The girls were all in line, waiting for their turn. When someone got their tail sticker on the donkey's tail, they got a prize out of the bucket. We played a few times, and Lauren didn't care if she won or lost, but she wanted to always be the one with the blindfold on. After a few times of redirecting her, she started getting upset. My anxiety level hit the roof. My mom was there to help, so I said, "Please take Lauren upstairs or outside." I was so afraid of her little friends seeing her have a tantrum. They were six now; not many of them had tantrums anymore, at least not for multiple hours.

Lauren was in full tantrum mode. I could hear her upstairs. The girls knew something was wrong. Mom came down and motioned for me to go upstairs. "I'll take over the party," she said.

Lauren was still mad, but she didn't know why at this point. I just had to wait for the gas to run out. Eventually, she would collapse from exhaustion. Lauren banged her head on the bed frame. I looked at her, perplexed.

"What on earth are you doing?" I asked.

She looked at me and hit her head again, this time with her fist.

"Lauren, stop that, you're going to hurt your—" I stopped dead in my sentence. She wanted to hurt herself. She didn't even know what that meant at six. I could see the idea ingrained in her mind. A piece of me died that day.

The last thing I wanted was to see a psychiatrist, but it was time. I knew Lauren needed more help than just a therapist or a counselor. The psychiatrist would be able to prescribe medication, and maybe we needed that.

WE WALKED INTO THE office. There were lots of books and little things to fidget with. I had never seen a psychiatrist, so I had no clue how this was done. We spent about an hour and a half going over every little detail of Lauren's life. What I hated the most was that I had to tell her story with her watching me. If I ever had the chance to do something over, that would be at the top of my list. I crushed her soul that day. I could see in her face that she was very sad.

After reviewing the records and our visit, the doctor decided that Lauren had depression, anxiety, and ADHD. So with careful thought and research, Lauren started on a mood stabilizer, an antidepressant, and an ADHD medication. We walked out of that appointment very shaken. I was trying to absorb what the doctor had said.

CHAPTER 12

GRADE SCHOOL WAS GETTING harder. In fourth grade, students switch from "learning to read" to "reading to learn." Lauren was falling behind academically. Socially, things were a nightmare. Kids were so mean and hurtful to Lauren that we decided to move to a different school district, one that we thought had a better program for Lauren. We packed up, sold our house, and moved to another house, another district. We were willing to do whatever it took to help Lauren. She had been so much brighter and happier a year ago, and now it seemed her eyes had lost their glow. I was seeing less and less of her dimples. Lauren was having more meltdowns, mostly at home. She was still holding it together at school, but because she was trying so hard to keep it together emotionally, she was having a hard time academically. We requested that she be tested by the special education department. We learned that she had a learning disability in math and a very slow processing speed. The teachers wanted to create an individualized education plan—an IEP—which would help them know the best way to help her in class.

As time went on, because of the emotional deregulation, Lauren was starting to have more emotional disruptions at school. She would cry if she didn't get math, or throw her pencil if she was frustrated. She was starting to disengage from the class and the teacher. Homework would just bring on the emotions and end in a meltdown at home. We did what we could and got by.

Summer came, and Lauren was thrilled to be free and wanted to be outside all the time. She connected with nature and animals. She told me, "The reason I love animals so much, Mom, is because they love you no matter what. They don't walk away or say mean things when they are mad."

That summer, we spent a lot of time at the pool. Nearby, there was a lot of chemical runoff from businesses near the small river that fed into the pond. Some of the frogs had three legs, and others had two heads. No one swam in the pond; it was just for looks. Lauren caught a frog and a tadpole every time we were at the pool. We had our own buckets and nets. When we pulled up to the pool, kids came running because they wanted to catch frogs with Lauren.

"Lauren, if you go down to the pond, you need to tell me," I said.

"I know, Mom," she said.

At the pool, I was doing everything *but* relaxing. Nikki was only five, so I was with her continuously. Megan was nine and could swim pretty well, and there were lifeguards, so I was able to let her go swim with friends. *Where is Lauren?* I thought.

This particular day, Lauren found herself a frog. She brought this frog over to me so I could see it. She was holding a twenty-ounce cup. She lifted the lid to show me. I couldn't see well enough, so I pulled the cup toward me. Out of the cup came a frog larger than any I had ever seen. It was the size of a small rabbit. I screamed and ran. I'd never had a problem being scared of animals, but this was something out of a science fiction movie. This frog was about a foot long with its legs extended. Lauren put the frog in a large bucket we had with us.

The afternoon started slipping away, and it was time to go home. We all piled into the minivan. I was gathering the towels and the thousand other things that we'd brought to the pool when I suddenly heard kids screaming. Not a scared or injured scream, but a scream of hysterical laughter. The frog had leapt out of the bucket and was in my car jumping freely. Nobody wanted to touch it except Lauren, and she was not about to let this fun end. Two male lifeguards had to jump and crawl through my car to catch this frog. When they got the frog back in the bucket, Lauren carried it over to me and, without saying a word, I pointed my finger at the pond. *I gave birth to Dennis the Menace*, I thought.

WHEN LAUREN WAS TWELVE, she wanted a lizard. "Mom, please can I get a bearded dragon?" She read me a laundry list of reasons they were cool.

"Lauren, I don't doubt they are very cool, but you don't have any supplies. It's really expensive to buy and care for a bearded dragon. Do you know how much it is?"

"I'll find out. Hang on," Lauren said. She hopped on the internet and looked everything up. "Mom, it comes to fifty-six dollars," she said proudly.

"Lauren, do you have fifty-six dollars?" I asked.

"No," she said sadly. "Hey, Mom, when I make fifty-six dollars, can I buy a bearded dragon?"

"Sure," I said. I unloaded the dishwasher and started making dinner. I thought that would appease her and I wouldn't have to listen to her whine about another animal. It would take her a long time to earn fifty-six dollars.

Half an hour later, Megan came into the kitchen. "Mom, is Lauren getting a bearded dragon?"

"What?" I had forgotten our conversation already. "Oh, yes, when she earns enough money," I joked. "Why do you ask?"

"She caught about ten frogs and turtles at the pond, and she's selling them to neighborhood kids."

I started laughing. Lauren was capable of much more than she was letting on. "I think we have a budding entrepreneur on our hands," I said to Jared.

By the end of the day, Lauren had made fifty dollars.

CHAPTER 13

"I DON'T HAVE ANYTHING to wear," Lauren cried.

"Why don't you wear that cute skirt and top grandma bought you?" I said.

Lauren pulled them out of her Mount Everest pile of clothes.

"How do you find anything in there?" I asked.

"Oh, this is cute," Lauren said, satisfied. Lauren and Megan had rooms on the lower level, and Nikki was across the hall from us. Megan was entering fifth grade. I always imagined that if I had girls, they would be perfect friends, especially if they were this close together in age. But Lauren and Megan couldn't be more different. Megan was starting to surpass Lauren academically and socially. In many ways, Megan acted much like the older sibling. This made situations tough when Megan had a good idea about something but Lauren pulled rank as big sister. None of this helped Lauren's self-esteem.

"I'm going to take Megan up to cheer practice," I said.

"Can I come too?" Lauren asked.

"Do you have homework?"

"I don't know," Lauren said, sounding bored.

How do you not know if you have homework? I thought. "Bring your backpack, and we'll look at your planner while Megan is at cheer."

All the kids in Lauren's sixth grade class were given a planner. Most of the time, the teachers told them what to write in the planner. Lauren's said: "Science test tomorrow."

I said, "This says you have a science test tomorrow."

"I do?" Lauren looked surprised.

"Did you bring your book home?"

"I bring all my books home, 'cause I don't know which ones I need," she said, unsure.

I opened her science book and asked Lauren which chapter the test was on.

"I don't know."

"Okay, what were you talking about in science?"

She looked at me blankly.

"Seriously, you don't know?" I started questioning her about other classes. She was all over the place, no organization. I hadn't paid much attention because, in grade school, they just came home with spelling words and read for fifteen minutes per day.

"Mom, I'm just stupid. I hate myself. Nobody likes me, you know. I want to die," she said.

"What? Lauren, die?" I tried to reassure her and help her understand she wasn't stupid.

"Why can't I be smart like Megan? Megan is perfect at everything." Lauren was getting mad, and people were starting to stare.

I closed my eyes. "Lauren, you have so many things you are good at too."

Megan came out from cheer practice and opened the van door.

"What's wrong with Lauren?" she asked.

"Shut up! Megan, I hate you," Lauren barked back.

"Okay, enough, both of you." I started driving home.

Megan started going on and on about cheer. "So I was in the middle of a tick up, and Sara didn't squeeze enough, and she fell. It was so bad. We were all embarrassed, and then coach made us do ten burpees. Coach wasn't happy, but—"

"Shut up, Megan," Lauren said. "No one cares."

"You shut up, Lauren. I hate you. I just want to tell Mom all about cheer and you're being mean. Seriously, be quiet."

"Make me," Lauren taunted.

Megan said something under her breath. At that moment Lauren lunged into the front seat and started hitting Megan. I swerved in the road, but I couldn't pull over because I was in the inside lane.

"Stop it, Lauren, now! Sit down!" I yelled.

"No! I hate you, Mom." Lauren opened the car door. "I'm going to jump out," she threatened. "I hate myself."

"Close the door." I was getting worried.

Lauren slammed the door shut. She started screaming and hitting her head on the seat. I drove as fast as I could home. Megan was sitting in the front seat crying, and when the car came to a stop she opened her door and ran inside. Lauren jumped into the passenger seat.

I was entirely out of my mind, freaking out at the behavior I'd just witnessed. "Lauren, I think you need help. You said you wanted to die. Do I need to take you to the hospital?"

"No, I do not want to go to the hospital."

"I think they can help us, help you." I started crying.

"This is so stupid. I hate you!" she screamed at me. She kicked her leg up onto the dash and proceeded to kick out the windshield.

I didn't know a person could kick out a windshield. This was all happening so fast. I felt like I was in a movie, watching myself to see what I should do next. This was not in the parent handbook. Lauren sat silently in the front seat. I blinked and sat silently, wondering exactly how I was going to tell Jared.

Jared came outside to see why Megan was so upset, with a look of *You're in trouble, young lady* and *Wow, I didn't know a person could kick out the windshield* all wrapped into one face. He walked to my side of the van and looked at me.

"I told Lauren that she needed to go to the behavioral hospital," I said. Jared nodded in agreement. Lauren sat emotionless. "Tell the girls I will be home in a few hours." It was already eight thirty; it was going to be a long night.

As I drove to the hospital, Lauren said, "Mommy, I'm sorry. I didn't mean to kick out the window. I just get so mad, and I don't know why."

"I know, Lauren, and that's what we need to figure out," I said.

We walked into the hospital and asked the front desk what we needed to do. This was the first in what would be a long line of hospitalizations and placements.

"What is she being seen for?" the lady asked.

"She wants to hurt herself, and she gets really mad sometimes."

"Go over there to the assessment desk; they can help you," she said.

We walked to the desk. There was a police officer sitting with a young girl who was handcuffed and, on the other side of her, a young man and an older woman. Everyone looked ragged and tired. Behind the desk, there were two security guards. "Boy, I would not want to mess up here," I said to Lauren. She took my arm and squeezed.

I filled out paperwork, and we waited until a tall, slender woman called for Lauren. We got up and walked to the designated room.

She closed the door. There were two doors—the one we came in and another on the opposite wall. I supposed that was an exit for if you were stuck in the room with someone and couldn't get out the other door. Scary.

The woman was friendly, very professional, and seemed to be in a good mood. I had never been in a psych hospital, and now I was leaving my daughter here. I couldn't hold back the tears.

"Mom, it's okay," said Lauren.

The woman handed me a tissue. "Lauren, what brings you in today?"

I looked at Lauren, not sure if she wanted to or even could explain what had happened. She looked panicked. I cleared my throat. "Is it okay if I answer?" I asked.

"Yes, that is just fine."

"Lauren was angry tonight over some homework. She and her sister got into a fight, and then Lauren tried to get out of the car while I was driving. She kicked the windshield out of my van. She said she hated herself and wanted to die. I've never heard her say that, and I was scared, so I decided to bring her in."

The woman typed as I was talking. When I mentioned the windshield, she looked up at me with big, concerned eyes. I answered questions about Lauren's medical history, birth, traumas, abuse, illnesses. Medical history of her sisters, mom, dad, and grandparents on both sides. I tried to figure out if they were going to keep her.

The woman said that we should wait while she called the doctor to get orders to admit Lauren tonight. When Megan was in the hospital with asthma problems, I never left her side. I was there to love and comfort my hurting child. Now Lauren was being hospitalized, and things were different. I had to leave her there. I could only see her for two hours a day. She couldn't wear shoes or a ponytail binder. She couldn't have a pencil or a pen in her room. *My baby*, I thought sadly.

The second door opened. "You can follow me," a nurse said. "How are you today?" she asked.

I forced a smiled and said, "I'm fine." I realized we hadn't packed anything before we came. I'd have to get stuff and bring it up later. Lauren was looking out the big windows in the hallway.

"Look, Mom, you can see the people that aren't locked in," she said matter-of-factly.

We stopped in front of a big door. "Here's the phone," the nurse said. "You just pick it up and tell the nurse who you are here for, and they'll give you a code number."

Okay, I thought. *That's probably a good thing, to keep things confidential.* She opened the heavy locked door, and we walked into the children's unit. *This isn't so bad,* I thought. The walls were painted different colors, and in the center there were about four tables with chairs. The cafeteria looked like a school lunchroom. Everyone had a private room. There was a bathroom, but staff had to unlock it for you. I looked in the bathroom mirror; it was like a metal cookie sheet. You could see yourself, but your reflection was distorted like a mirror in a fun house. All the doors opened from either direction. The shower curtain was on a safety cord. If you tugged a little, the whole curtain would come down. The beds were a platform, a mattress, one pillow, one sheet, and a blanket. The hospital provided clothing, pajamas, and hygiene items. The kids got a tray of food three times a day, as well as afternoon and nighttime snacks. After dinner, if you did everything you were supposed to do that day, you got to watch a movie in the cafeteria with the other kids. If not, you showered and went to bed.

We were escorted to Lauren's room. It was at the end of the hallway, next door to a schoolroom. We didn't have anything to put away, so we just sat on her bed and looked at each other.

"Lauren, are you okay?" I asked her, not sure what to say or how to say it.

"I'm fine." She wasn't mad or fighting to get out. She was like one of the frogs she used to catch and put in buckets, not a bit of struggle—she knew she wasn't going anywhere.

"Kari, can you please come and fill out some paperwork?" a nurse asked me.

I walked into the conference room, and the nurse directed me to the forms I had to fill out. There were basic questions about allergies and approved visitors as well as two assessments for different mental health issues in separate packets. *I'll be here until one in the morning*, I thought.

Once I had everything filled out, I had to watch a welcome video for orientation to the unit. I walked to the nurses' station and asked what I should do with my forms.

"I'll take those," the receptionist said. She was putting Lauren's chart together. I saw Lauren sitting in a chair, looking drained. I slowly walked up to her and put my hand on her shoulder.

"Do you remember the story in the Bible that talks about the Kingdom of Heaven?" I said.

"Yeah?"

"You know that the Kingdom is always there, has always been there, and will be there forever and ever?"

She nodded.

"You know what else?"

"What?" Lauren looked at me with big brown eyes.

"It's already been given to us."

"Really?" She was so happy. I smiled and nodded.

"I know God put you on this earth with some tough things to deal with. It is not easy or fair to be born with a disability. God chooses those people special because he knows they can handle it. God has given you the power to get through it. All you need to do is find out how and forge through."

Lauren looked somewhat peaceful.

"You just have to remember that promise and where you will be, someday." I kissed her forehead, hugged her tight, and said good-bye. I was trying to keep it together. I took all the papers, codes, and pamphlets and folded them together so it was easier to hold. I looked back at Lauren and slowly waved goodbye. I walked out the big door that locked, into the long hallway with the windows. *Click.*

It was about one in the morning. I went through two more locked doors and then out into the lobby. There were people waiting to be seen, some accompanied by police. I continued walking out the main automatic sliding doors, past three police cars and a man smoking on the sidewalk. I got in my car, took a deep breath, and cried like I'd never cried before.

This was what she was looking at for the next fifty years; this was her life now. This was our life now.

CHAPTER 14

OUR TOWN WAS GROWING rapidly, and the district needed to build a new middle school. "I was thinking," I said to Jared as we were getting ready for bed. "Do you think the district would allow Lauren to stay at East Middle School?" Lauren didn't do well with change, and some of the girls who were going to the new middle school were pretty nasty. Lauren struggled socially, but those girls made it unbearable.

"Yeah, that's a great idea," Jared said.

"I'll call Krystal and ask her what we need to do." Working in the special education department, Krystal was probably used to these requests. I called their office and pleaded my case.

"You will need to have a meeting with the superintendent regarding school placement. That may be something we can write in her IEP," the assistant to the superintendent explained.

"Okay, good. Let's set that up," I said, relieved.

Having an appointment with the superintendent was unnerving. I parked the car, and Jared and I walked to the main entrance.

He held the door for me.

"Thank you, sir," I said with a wink, trying to be funny. Krystal was waiting for us right outside the door that led into the central office.

"Hi, guys," she said with a smile. She was always so easy to talk to, very compassionate and down to earth. "Do you have what you need? Mr. Beckholm is ready if you are," she said, guiding us to the meeting room. We met in his office, a large room with stacks of books and some papers on the desk. There were pictures of his family in frames on the shelf. We sat at a big, long table at the other end of the office.

"Can I get you some coffee, water, or soda?"

"I'm good." I looked at Jared.

"No, but thank you," Jared said.

Mr. Beckholm started. "I believe we're here today to talk about Lauren and her desire to stay at East Middle School, is that right?"

"Yes, that is correct," I said, feeling very timid.

"We are very strict about our school district and the boundaries," he said. "I'm not a fan of her going to a school outside of her designated boundary."

My heart deflated. *What am I going to do?* I thought.

"However," Mr. Beckholm continued, "it was brought to my attention that Lauren struggles with school and that the West Middle School girls are a trigger for her."

"That's correct," Jared piped up.

"Lauren has been hospitalized at the Behavioral Center for suicidal thoughts, right?"

"Yes, and I have her records here with me," I said.

"Okay, thanks. Give them to Krystal," he said, nodding to her.

"We can put those in her file if you'd like," Krystal said.

"Based on what I see," Mr. Beckholm said, "I am going to grant you permission to have Lauren attend East Middle School." He turned to Krystal. "Will you get that written in her IEP?"

"Yes, that shouldn't be a problem," Krystal said.

"Thank you for meeting with us," Jared said. "We do appreciate it." Jared shook Mr. Beckholm's hand. We walked out of the office and into the lobby area.

"I'll be in touch, and we'll get the IEP meeting set up," Krystal said.

"Sounds good, Krystal. Thanks for meeting with us," I said.

Jared and I walked to the car. "Well, that's over," I said in relief. "I don't know why I was so nervous. He seems like a nice guy. I hope having her stay at East works out okay."

"It will work out. It has to," Jared said.

LAUREN WAS READY FOR seventh grade, and volleyball season started up. "Lauren, you sure you want to play volleyball?" I asked her. I wanted her in something extracurricular, and I didn't care what.

"Yeah, volleyball sounds good. I think some of my friends are playing too," Lauren said.

I don't know who she's referring to, but we'll go with it, I thought.

There were four teams, ranked A through D. Lauren made the C team. "Congrats, Lauren," I told her, as I was standing in the back of the gym with the other moms.

"Mom, these girls are coming to our house to hang out and try on dresses for the dance. Oh, yeah, there is a dance after orientation." Lauren had never been interested in dances, and I was a little hesitant, but Lauren has such a hard time making and keeping friends that I sometimes let things slide. Seventh grade was a big year, and I wanted so much for it to go well for her. Maybe this would help her start on the right foot.

"Okay, sure," I said. Lauren and the girls hopped in the car. I knew Kara and Lyndsey, but Faith was new. "Nice to meet you," I said.

"Do you think we can order pizza?" I heard one of the girls ask.

"Mom, can we order pizza?"

"I don't see why not," I said, feeling a little annoyed. "When do you girls have to be home?"

"I don't know. We'll let you know."

"Okay," I said, confused.

The girls went to Lauren's room and tried on dresses. They ate pizza and seemed to have a good time. About eight, I figured I should take the girls home. None of the parents were willing to come pick up their children; Lauren had a way of picking friends who came from tougher walks of life and whose parents didn't appear to be that involved. The kids fended for themselves. I wanted so badly for this night to go well with her that I didn't complain about the inconvenience.

Seventh grade was starting off well. Lauren had her locker figured out and knew where her classes were. We went to orientation for parents and students, and Lauren seemed like she knew what was going on. We walked from class to class. A few kids talked to her. Kara, Lyndsey, and Faith were hanging out by a locker.

"Mom, I'm going to talk to my friends," she said, and walked toward them.

Lauren uses the term friends very loosely, I thought. While I waited, I struck up a conversation with an old college friend that I hadn't seen in a decade.

"Mom," Lauren tapped me on the shoulder.

I put my pointer finger up as to say *just gimme a minute.*

"Mom," Lauren said.

I paused. "Yes, Lauren."

"So my friends want to come over and get ready at my house for the dance. Is that okay?"

My gut was questioning these friends, but how could I have said no? She'd never had anyone want to get ready for a dance with her. *She seems so happy. I need to stop worrying,* I thought. We all piled into the car.

The girls only had an hour to get ready. "Girls," I said, "you go downstairs and get dressed. I'll make a few sandwiches so you will have something to eat before the dance." I could hear music and girls giggling.

The girls came up to the kitchen and ate the sandwiches. "Okay, I'll drop you off at the dance. Call me when you are ready to come back here."

"They're going to sleep over. Is that okay?" Lauren said.

I rolled my eyes. I didn't know if a sleepover was a great idea, but I was trying to make this work.

The girls looked beautiful. They had on dresses and nice shoes. Their hair was done up cute, with pins and hairspray. I drove to the middle school gym entrance. "Okay," I said, "please stay together. No leaving school grounds, and please make good choices."

They all stared at me. I'd figured their parents had given them this advice before, but they were apparently hearing it for the first time. They closed the doors and walked into the gym. I drove home, nervous, trying not to look at the school in the rearview mirror.

I was trying to carve some time out for Megan and Nikki. Nikki and I decided to play a quick, little card game. I think it was called "garbage."

My cell phone rang. "Hello," I said timidly.

"Mom, come and get me! I hate everyone."

So my anxiety had been justified. "Jared, I need to go up to the middle school. Lauren called and wants to come home. I'll be back soon, I hope. I'm sorry, Nikki."

Lauren was waiting by the glass doors at the entrance of the school. She was crying, and kids were staring at her. "What's wrong?" I asked.

"Some boys said I was big and that I would never have a boyfriend."

Here we go. Welcome to middle school. I tried to console Lauren and listen to her. Kids were starting to whisper. She had seen the boys again while she was waiting and yelled that they were stupid and that she hated them, and the boys laughed. I saw Kara, Lyndsey, and Faith standing together in the gym. I motioned for them to talk to me. "Hi, girls. Do you know what's going on?" The girls just looked at me. They were not going to tell me anything. "I'm taking Lauren home," I said. "Can you all call your parents and let them know that you need a ride home, please? Tell them Lauren is ill. Let me know if you don't get ahold of them."

I was sad that it didn't go well, but I was relieved that I wasn't going to have three girls that I hardly knew staying overnight. When walked in the door, Megan was crying. "Lauren," she yelled. "Where is my new tank top, my new sports bra, and my American Eagle shorts? Nikki said your friend was wearing them."

Lauren looked dumbfounded. Clothes were not a big deal to Lauren. "I told Kara she could wear something of yours since she and you are about the same size. I guess she was wearing the clothes when we were getting ready. She said she was going to change at the gym." As Lauren explained, she realized that it really didn't make much sense.

"They were brand new, and I hadn't even worn them!"

"Megan," I said, "I know you are mad, but calm down. Let's text Kara and see if she has the clothes. I'll ask her to drop them off after the dance on her way home."

"Mom, I know kids. She'll go home and forget about the clothes in her bag. Then, when I ask for them, she'll say, 'Okay, I'll bring it tomorrow.' And finally she'll just forget about it. What am I supposed to do then, search her room? No, I'm just out a new outfit that I paid for with my own money."

I had Lauren text Kara and ask her to please bring the clothes back to our house after the dance. Kara texted back "ok" and then didn't answer any more texts. At ten, half an hour after the dance ended, I had Lauren call Kara. She said she was home and that she forgot.

I thought Jared was going to pop an artery. "No, they need to come back to our house and bring back Megan's clothes."

"We asked them to do that," said Lauren. "It's not my fault she forgot."

"Well this is a great way to start the year," I grumbled. I put my head in my hands, covering my face.

Eventually, the doorbell rang. Kara was delivering the clothes, and she looked mad. Jared went out the car to thank the parent and explain the situation. When he walked out there, he got an earful of parenting advice.

"Well, she was not very happy," he said as he walked back in the house.

"I've never met any of the parents," I said, feeling like I needed to defend myself. "I've only seen them at volleyball practice."

"It's always some drama. I'm going to bed." He walked down the hall to the bedroom and shut the door.

CHAPTER 15

"MEGAN, DID YOU GET your stuff in the car?" I asked. "The bus leaves at seven forty-five." Megan was in competitive cheer, and their gym was the best in the state. This weekend was their first big competition, and it was in Chicago. Cheer was something that Megan got to do with me, alone, and she looked forward to Mom time. "I know it's hard," I said to Nikki, and kissed her. "I'll be home in two days. This weekend, you, Lauren, and Daddy are going to the apple festival."

Her eyes lit up. "Okay, Mommy."

Lauren had been following me all afternoon. "Mom, don't leave. Please don't leave."

"Lauren, I am going to cheer, and Daddy is home. You will be okay."

"Mom!" she yelled. "I don't want you to go."

I sat down with her on the couch, thinking that maybe she just needed a few Mom minutes. "I'm going to be home soon. This is a quick there-and-back competition."

"Yeah, but Megan gets to go."

I took a deep breath. "Lauren, you know Megan is performing."

"I want to go too," Lauren whined.

"Lauren, you have tried going to these competitions. You don't like them because they are loud and busy. You will be so much happier here."

"It's not fair. I want to go," she clung to me, crying hard.

What is going on with you, child? I thought.

"Mom, we have to go," Megan said.

"Okay, get in the car, start it, and I'll be right there."

"No, Mom, you're not going," Lauren moaned.

We were running out of time; the bus was going to leave without us. "Lauren, what if I brought you something?" I said, trying to bribe her. I looked over at Jared.

"Don't look at me," he said, and shrugged.

We were starting to not see eye-to-eye on the Lauren behavior plan. Jared would say, "I'm leaving," and walk out the door, not trying to make her unhappy, but not wanting to be late. I, on the other hand, wanted to make sure she understood that I was coming back, that I would call her, that Daddy was home to take care of her. I mostly wanted her to calm down for Jared and Nikki's sake. I would still usually get a call from Lauren about every hour, complaining about something. Then Jared would get on her about calling me so much, and I'd spend the rest of the trip with anxiety about how things were going. Jared and I would end up in a squabble because I was micromanaging from far away and he wanted me to let him handle it, and that would make my anxiety even worse.

"Mom, we're going to be late!" Megan yelled from the garage door.

I was in a full-on sweat at this point. Jared had to hold Lauren while I peeled her hands off my shirt. I walked out the door and cried all the way to the cheer bus.

"Huh, what a great way to start off a cheer trip, Mom," Megan said. I didn't want to socialize with all the happy cheer moms. I just wanted to sit alone and look out the window.

School was now in full swing, and Lauren was at East Middle School, as we planned with the superintendent. The friend debacle was behind us. Lauren was in and out of the behavioral hospital. We had fall events, and the clubs were starting to meet. Lauren wanted to do drama. She could sing pretty well, but I thought she might be more interested in working behind the scenes, making the props.

As we drove to school every day, we talked about how to make that day a good one. We talked about visiting with people and not saying anything mean or hurtful. We talked about respecting teachers and bringing homework home. Every day, the same conversation. Every day, the same drama.

"I want to go to meet Jesus," Lauren said one day as we were driving to school.

I swallowed hard. "Um, what do you mean?" I said.

She looked down. "God made me, and Jesus loves me, so I want to go to heaven. Jesus will be my friend. I know he will. He promised."

I took a deep breath. I wanted to sucker punch all the people who were ever mean to my child. "Lauren," I said, "you would have to die to go to heaven and see Jesus."

"I know, Mom," she said matter-of-factly. A horrible twang of dread went through my body from head to toe.

We arrived at school, and Lauren got out and started walking into school. "Hey," I yelled to her. She looked back at me, super annoyed. "I love you." I tried to say it without embarrassing her.

"Yep, I know, Mom. You have to, 'cause you're my mom." She was emotionless. She went through the doors and melted in with the crowd.

I looked out into the parking lot. In the distance, I could see corn and beans getting ready to be harvested. The sun was out, and the sky was a bright blue color. The temperature was sixty degrees, and there was a little breeze. The air smelled like leaves and morning dew. Kids and parents were hustling to start their day. And my daughter wanted to die.

I decided to go into the office and talk to a counselor. I opened the school doors and immediately smelled the school odor of glue and books.

"Hello, Mrs. Gusso. How can I help you today?"

I hated that they knew my name. I don't think my principal even knew who my mom was; she never had to come to school. "Can I talk to the counselor? It's about Lauren."

"She's out today. Do you want to talk to the assistant principal instead?"

"Yes, please," I said.

Lauren had been having some behavior issues: wanting to go to the nurse, not coming to school, yelling and swearing at kids in the hall, and crying in class. Homework was getting to be a major nightmare. Jared and I had daily battles with Lauren over homework, and we didn't even get it done most nights. Nikki and Megan were on their own; I tried to answer a question here and there, but every ounce of energy went into getting Lauren's homework done and getting through the evening.

Bathing had become a power struggle. Lauren hated taking baths, washing her hair, and brushing her teeth. She had braces, and the orthodontist was about to the point of taking them off because they were so bad and ruining her teeth from no brushing.

"Hi, Kari," the assistant principal said. He took me to his office. "What's going on?" he said. He knew me and Lauren well. She spent about an hour a day in his office, and he had me on speed dial. I usually ended up going up to the school to get her.

"Well," I said, "Lauren said something to me today when I dropped her off about wanting to be dead. I just wanted you and the school to be aware."

He looked at me; he didn't know how to respond. "I'm so sorry," he said finally.

I didn't know what I was expecting him to do. "I just didn't know where to go." We had a friendly conversation, and as always I left feeling like I'd gotten no help for my daughter.

Lauren tried to fit in, talking to people at lunch and in classes, but she was very isolated. The girls from the dance talked to Lauren, but unless they wanted something from her they pretty much left her alone. No one called. Lauren's friends consisted of the three-year-old twins across the street, Grandma Jane, and Molly, our dog. Lauren would sometimes ask if she could have a friend over, and I never knew how to respond. If I said okay, she would call twenty people, and everyone would say they were busy.

Lauren spent a lot of time with my parents, who lived about a mile from us. She rode her bike over to their house when she was bored, sad, or angry. Lauren and my mom had a special bond, and I was so thankful for that. Lauren could open up to Grandma Jane. Although my parents had spent a lot of time with Lauren, they hadn't witnessed many of her really bad meltdowns.

My mom called and asked if Lauren was home.

"No . . ." *What now?* I thought. We had just arrived home from conferences at the grade school with Nikki. "What happened?"

"Well," Mom started, "I really am not sure what happened. Lauren had come over, she was visiting with Katie and the boys.

They were talking about Lauren and the plan for her to stay the night with us tonight. Lauren mentioned that she wanted to go up to the school where you and Jared were for conferences. We told her no and she got mad and went anyway. We did tell her that if she went, there would be no sleepover. Lauren went anyway."

"We never saw her," I said.

"Well, she came back and was upset when we told her the consequences. She was on the driveway and yelling some pretty nasty words at Grandpa Ken. She went from zero to a hundred in about six seconds. Our neighbors were outside, and it was really embarrassing. I just don't know what you are going to do with her."

"Okay, stop," I said, annoyed. I don't know why I got defensive. "I will come get her now." I hung up the phone, got into my van, and drove the half mile to my parents' house. I pulled up near the driveway, and Lauren jumped in. My parents and sister were standing there looking at me, like I was supposed to get out of the car and explain myself in an hour-long conversation about how this could've gone better. I didn't have the energy to do this. It wasn't that I didn't care, but I was so tired of every situation that Lauren was involved in ending in some kind of catastrophe. I needed to go home and process this. My mind was spinning.

Mornings were unbearable. "Lauren, you need to get up," I said as I was nudging her gently in bed. "We have to leave in ten minutes." I walked out of her room. "I've been trying to wake her up for about forty-five minutes now," I said to Jared. "She won't budge. She's awake, she just doesn't want to get up and go to school."

Jared was getting frustrated. "Lauren, you need to get up now, or you're grounded to the house today after school."

"Jared." I looked at him with total frustration. "Just take Megan and Nikki to school. I'll get Lauren going, hopefully." I could tell that Megan and Nikki were upset and scared.

Lauren managed to get up and put on clothes. Once Lauren was awake and up, she was okay. She ate breakfast, and we were on our way. "Bye, Mom. I guess I'll see you after school." She seemed like she was actually in a good mood. When she smiled, her brown eyes lit up and I could see her dimples.

I hadn't showered, but I needed to run some errands. By the time I had made it to the grocery store, my phone started vibrating. The school district's number came across my screen.

"Hello," I said, not wanting to hear what was going on.

"Hi, this is Mary, the school nurse at East Middle School. Lauren would like to talk to you."

Okay, I thought. *This is different.*

"Mommy," Lauren said, crying. "A boy cut my hair."

"What—what do you mean?" I was confused.

"They were making fun of me, and a boy was pretending to cut my hair, and then he did."

"How much did he cut?" I asked, but I wasn't concerned about her hair; I was more concerned with what happened.

The nurse got back on the phone. "Hi, Kari—"

"Hi," I interrupted. "What happened? Scissors? Where was the teacher? Who did this? I hope there is a consequence for this kid."

The nurse stumbled over her words.

"I'm on my way to the school now." I hung up the phone and called Jared. "Hey, meet me at the middle school," I said, barely explaining what had happened. He was in a meeting and had to duck out early. I was furious now. How dare some kid come at my child with scissors, and then actually cut her hair? Where was the teacher?

Lauren was in the nurses' station when I arrived. Jared arrived shortly behind me, and we were escorted to the principal's office.

"Have a seat," he said. He explained to us what had happened, and didn't seem too concerned. "The boy didn't mean to cut her hair. It was an accident."

I looked at Jared. I blinked three times, took a deep breath, cleared my throat, and stood up. Calmly, I said, "My daughter was assaulted today with scissors at the school that you are in charge of. The other child used the scissors to harm my child. My child was being made fun of for whatever reason, and your teacher apparently did not know what was going on in her classroom. You are telling me that it was an accident." I stared at him. "Seriously, this is going to be swept under the rug? What happened to zero tolerance?"

Jared and I walked back to the lobby. I took Lauren's hand and walked out of the building.

We were getting no academic or psychological help for Lauren at the public school. We'd been told that every child deserved a free and appropriate education—except, apparently, Lauren. I didn't know if I'd done the right thing or not. I was mostly pissed about the fact that the boys were well-liked and popular. It was funny to them. But Lauren was not going to be the butt of their jokes anymore. I had been to middle school and high school. I knew the crap that went on behind closed doors. I had a classmate commit suicide because of it. I couldn't let that to happen to my daughter.

"Lauren," I said, "how do you feel about Catholic school?"

CHAPTER 16

I GREW UP IN a Catholic home, and I went to Catholic school for twelve years. I wanted the girls to go too, but at the time they started school, we just didn't have the money for tuition. It's funny how you can scrounge up tuition money when you really need it.

We walked up to the door and rang the bell. There were cameras pointing at us. The door clicked, and we walked in.

"Hi, can I help you?" said an older woman at the desk.

"We want to enroll our daughter at this school," I said, trying to sound confident and not like a complete idiot.

"All right, please fill out these papers. I will let the principal, Mr. Knight, know that you are here."

The girls were baptized Catholic, but we had started attending a Baptist church that we fell in love with here in our town. The girls didn't have their first communion in the Catholic church. "Do I mark that we're Catholic?" I asked Jared in a whisper.

Jared looked at me big eyes, shaking his head. "I have no idea," he whispered back.

"Why do I feel like we're trying to get away with something?" I marked *yes*. Lauren was sitting in her chair eating a Subway sandwich. She had missed lunch.

Mr. Knight called us into his office. He was about thirty-five years old and very nice—easy to talk to, compassionate, and willing to help us. We explained the whole school situation. He didn't seem surprised. "Sometimes kids just need a fresh start," he explained.

I was thrilled he felt this way. We met with special ed and counselors to put together a plan. Private schools didn't have the rules that governed an IEP. They followed it; it was just a little different format. Lauren had accommodations for a math learning disability, ADHD, and emotional issues. I was so happy that these teachers were willing to do what they could to help Lauren.

Lauren jumped in and did great at the school. Soon after starting, she called me from school and asked if she could go home with a girl, Hope, after school.

"Did she invite you?" I asked. *What a dumb question*, I thought after I said it out loud.

"Yes, she is super sweet. She's in cheer with Megan."

"Oh, I know Hope. Yes, you can go. Call and let me know when I should come pick you up." *We did the right thing,* I thought.

"I NEED RED AND blue paper, glitter glue, and popsicle sticks," Lauren said excitedly after school one day. I was thrilled she was doing homework on her own.

"What are you making?" I asked.

She was at the kitchen table building and gluing, concentrating so hard her tongue was sticking out a little. "It's a Viking ship. We are Scandinavian, and the teacher wants us to build a boat with our heritage showing. So I'm doing a Viking ship," she said proudly.

"Great idea, Lauren."

Nikki was elbow deep in glue and glitter, helping her big sister and making a Disney-themed boat of her own.

Lauren started St. Paul's in October. She met some girls, and they went skiing and sledding and did other fun things. She occasionally talked on the phone. I had a feeling this was too good to be true, and I held my breath.

Little by little, Lauren started having trouble with academics. This spiraled into extra homework time, which fell into meltdowns at home. A very unhappy Lauren would then go to school under duress. It turned miserable for everyone. The kids tried to be kind to Lauren. They tried helping her study, and they wanted to help her keep calm. Then, little by little, the phone calls started. The secretary was getting annoyed with her. Teachers were at their wits' end. Lauren was talkative in class, wasn't respectful, didn't do her homework, and had a few meltdowns.

Jared and I had met with Mr. Knight multiple times, trying to figure out what to do to help Lauren. We were now seeing him far more frequently. When Lauren was agitated and in a meltdown state, she came unglued. We were used this, but nobody else was.

Apparently, some boys started poking fun at her, and she'd had it. Lauren sat down in the hallway, crying and flustered. She yelled in the hall full of sixth and seventh graders, "Fuck you! I hate you assholes." This didn't fly in a Catholic middle school.

So on a cold, very snowy December day, I got a call from the secretary. "Mr. Knight would like to see you in his office." I called Jared.

"Yeah, I got the same call," he said. "What's going on?"

"I have no idea. I'll meet you there, I guess."

I was sitting in the folding chair when Jared walked into the office. We were covered in snow; it was getting to be a blizzard outside. "You may go in now," the secretary said to us, pointing to Mr. Knight's office. We walked in and took our seats. The special ed teacher was there too. *Oh boy, this doesn't look very good,* I thought.

Mr. Knight cleared his throat. "Never in my years of teaching have I ever had a student like Lauren." I thought I could see tears in his eyes. "She is disrespectful to the kids and also to the staff. She yells profanity in the hallway when she is mad, and she refuses to do anything we tell her. She won't do schoolwork, and when she does do work, it is done poorly. I'm sorry, but she is completely distracting these kids. I'm going to have to ask her to leave St. Paul's."

"Okay," I said. Honestly, I had expected this. But I was still mortified. I gathered up Lauren and all the school supplies we bought specially for her new school. "I have never been yelled at by a principal before," I said to Jared as we were walking out to the car.

Jared laughed but also sounded afraid. "Me neither."

"What the heck are we supposed to do?" I said to Jared. "She was at St. Paul's for three months; I'm going to have to call Krystal and let her know our situation. They have to help us; they're our school district. They have to take her back, right?" I had a headache.

"Krystal, this is Kari Gusso. How are you?"

"I'm driving through a blizzard. How much snow are we going to get?" she said, sounding muffled.

"I don't know, but it's coming down. Do you want to call me back when you are at your office?" I asked.

"Yeah, let me do that," she said. The weather wasn't great; roads were getting slick. There were probably seven inches of snow already. Jared, Lauren, and I went to grab a bite and waited for Krystal to call.

I took a drink of creamy hot chocolate. "Are you okay?" I asked

Jared. He looked as though he'd been tackled by the first-line foot-ball players. He gave me a slight smirk. My cell phone rang loudly and I jumped in my seat. "Hello," I said timidly.

"Hi, Kari. What's up?"

I started talking, not knowing where to start. "You probably know we went to St. Paul's in October."

"I did hear that. How is she doing?" Krystal asked.

I paused. "Lauren has been sliding for a while. She did well at first but then started to decline, both academically and emotion-ally." I paused again; I didn't want to say it. "She was asked to leave." A tear dripped down my cheek. "What are we supposed to do now?"

"Oh, Kari, I'm so sorry. This must be so hard for you and Jared. I was just thinking about Lauren the other day," Krystal explained. "I was at a special school called Child's Place; it is a K–8 school for kids with emotional and behavioral disorders."

I looked at Jared with concern.

"I think Lauren would do well there; I don't know why I didn't think of this earlier. I know they have a spot open. Do you want to tour the facility? I'm free this afternoon," she offered.

"That would be great." I took another sip of hot chocolate. I looked at the snow falling on the cars, covering them like a blanket. "We'll meet you there."

CHAPTER 17

LAUREN, JARED, AND I finished eating and started driving to Child's Place. It wasn't too far as the crow flies, but driving there was a trek.

"Mom, I'm kinda scared to look at this school. Are you going to leave me here?" Lauren said as she took off her earbuds, gently rolled them up, and put them in her bag.

"No, Lauren, we are just going to look at it and take a tour." I put one foot on the ground, stepping out of the car carefully. There were about eight inches now. *This is a regular aerobic workout,* I thought as we stomped through the snow in our boots. I was getting hot in my jacket.

We walked into a building that had two sets of glass doors. There was a foyer that had a phone, and I picked it up. It rang several times with no answer. Lauren was getting restless, so she and Jared went to look at animal prints in the snow. Krystal was here, walking toward us on what had been the sidewalk but was now covered up with snow. "Walk at your own risk," I said, laughing.

"I'm hoping not to catch the edge of the uneven sidewalk," Krystal said. She came and waited in the foyer with me. Jared and Lauren continued to blow off steam in the snow. I picked up the phone again.

"Hello, Child's Place. Can I help you?" a young woman said.

"We're here for a tour," Krystal said. The door clicked, and we walked in. A wave of sadness came over me. How many times had I heard that click? The click that let you know without a doubt that you were either locked in or locked out. I felt as though I was part of a club now, a club that I didn't want or plan to be in.

We walked into the lobby. I waved to Jared and Lauren to come back in. The lobby was cozy, more like a living room in a house than a lobby in a big public school.

"Betty will be with you in a minute," the girl said.

I sat down on the couch. I felt more assured that this would be a good fit for Lauren. It had already been such a long, horrible day; I was still reeling from getting yelled at for Lauren's behavior at St. Paul's. "I feel like our options are dwindling," I quietly told Krystal.

Lauren and Jared rang the bell; then came the click. "Mom, Dad said those tracks in the snow were from a deer."

"Cool, Lauren." I tried to sound excited.

A well-dressed, slightly overweight woman walked into the lobby. "Hi, I'm Betty. I hear you'd like a tour?" Krystal stepped forward. "Hi, Krystal. How are you?" Betty and Krystal knew each other from many previous placements, and they appeared to have a good relationship. "Is this Lauren?" she asked very calmly. "Hi, Lauren. I understand you want to see our school."

Lauren looked at me with a smirk. "My mom and dad do," she said.

"What grade are you in?"

Lauren looked at me so I could answer. I tried to get her to answer for herself.

"She is in seventh grade," I said after a long pause.

"Let's look at the junior high wing," Betty said. She started walking, and we all followed like chicks trailing after the mama duck.

As we walked down the hallway, I could sense that this was a very caring place. As we passed each room, I saw kids talking and laughing, teachers teaching, students watching a video. I didn't hear yelling or crying. I could tell that some of these kids had some mental delays, and a few were in wheelchairs or used walkers. Betty turned and looked at us. I think she could sense what we were thinking. "There are about two hundred kids here at Child's Place. Most of them live here because they can't be placed in a foster home. Some kids are here two weeks, and others have been here for years. We try to make it feel like home. We also have the day school, which is what Lauren would be doing." She knocked gently and walked into a room; the teacher came to meet us. "Hi, Mrs. Anderson. This is Lauren. She might be joining the seventh graders here at Child's Place."

Mrs. Anderson looked at Lauren and held her hand out. "Nice to meet you, Lauren."

Lauren looked at me, wondering what she should do.

"It's okay. You can shake her hand," I said to Lauren. I was getting worried that she would think everyone was out to get her.

After we toured the rest of the building, we walked back to our car. The snow had let up and the sun was peeking through the clouds. Krystal was talking, but all I could do was look at the freshly fallen snow. It glistened in the sun, like diamonds.

"Kari, is that the plan?" Jared pulled me out of my daze.

"Huh, what?"

Jared looked at me funny. He winked. Everyone chuckled. I was emotionally exhausted.

"Yes, Lauren will start Monday, the busing is arranged, and they have her IEP and school records."

"Great," Krystal said, brushing the snow off her car with a broom. "It's all I had," she said, and laughed. "See you soon, Kari and Jared. Bye, Lauren. We'll see you Monday."

Lauren gave one nod and got in the car.

I was in the kitchen, trying to make breakfast for everyone. I was so tired. "Mondays are so painful," I said as I tried to drown myself in coffee. I was always so tired. And I was tired of being so tired. Lauren was getting her shoes on and seemed excited to go to school. I was thrilled and relieved, but still cautious. The wheels fell off all the time; why would this time be any different? The girls were all getting ready for school, but nobody was talking. Everyone was in their own little world.

Megan jumped up. "I have to go. My bus will be here soon."

"Nikki, get in Dad's car. He'll take you to school today."

"Okay," she said as she ran to brush her teeth.

"Don't forget your lunch."

"Got it, Mom." Nikki said with a mouth full of toothpaste. Lauren and I stood by the door waiting for her bus.

"I wonder what the bus will look like," Lauren said. Just then, a tan minivan pulled into the driveway. There were no other kids on it.

"Go ahead and get in, Lauren." I motioned her to get in the passenger seat.

"Hi, you must be Kari. I'm Frances," the driver said, smiling. "I am one of the aides at Child's Place, but I also drive the van to and from school. You're my first pickup, and we'll get three more after you."

I nodded to Lauren to say that this was okay. "Bye, Lauren. Have a good day." She smiled at me. I watched the van back down the driveway. *Please let this work,* I prayed. *It has to.*

Lauren seemed to do well for about the first two weeks. She always had a honeymoon period in which she followed the rules and her behavior was great. Then the wheels fell off.

"Mom, could you help me with my math?" Megan said, sitting at the kitchen bar. Nikki was watching a cartoon and relaxing on the couch. I sat at the kitchen bar next to Megan. She was reading a problem when Lauren bolted in the house.

I jumped. "Hi, Lauren. How was your day?" I asked, not sure what kind of answer I would get.

"Mom, I hate school," Lauren said. "It's so dumb. I don't get any of it." She went on and on.

"Shut up, Lauren!" Megan yelled.

Lauren turned her head slowly, like a lion ready to pounce. "Whatever, Megan. Shut the fuck up," Lauren said to her very calmly.

"Girls!" I yelled. "This behavior is not okay."

"Yeah, but Lauren can't help it," Megan mumbled under her breath.

"Go to hell, Megan. I hate you," Lauren said as she walked toward Megan. Lauren had tried to scare Megan in the past. I worried about Lauren hurting her. Lauren was bigger and stronger, and even more so when she was mad.

I got between the girls and put my arm out. "Lauren, go to your room," I said.

"No," Lauren said. "I'm gonna hit you so hard, Megan."

"Oh, okay, Lauren. I'd like to see you try," Megan taunted.

Lauren tried to push me aside. "Lauren, stop, please," I said. I saw Nikki get up and run to her room, which she usually did when

Lauren was mad like this.

Megan ran to the other side of the table.

"I'm gonna get you, Megan," Lauren said.

"Lauren, stop now!" I yelled. I was pushed up against Megan. Lauren was pushed up against me. Lauren's arm flew past me and nailed Megan in the upper arm.

"Ow!" Megan said, now crying. "I hate you, Lauren," she screamed. "Why do you have to be so dumb?"

Lauren took another swing at Megan; this time, she hit her in the mouth.

"Aaahhhhh," Megan screamed.

"Ha, take that," Lauren said.

Megan bolted to her room downstairs. "I hate you, Lauren! Why do you have to ruin everything?"

I held Lauren back. "Stupid Megan," she said, walked into her room, and slammed the door.

Lauren's room had been downstairs until about a year prior; we'd decided to move her upstairs for safety reasons. Megan and Lauren were always fighting; it got so bad we couldn't trust them downstairs alone. Mostly we couldn't trust that Lauren wouldn't hurt her sister. There seemed to be more and more days like this lately.

I started to see Megan drifting away, going to friends' houses, and retreating to her room. Nikki was also hiding in her room, uncomfortable around the yelling and fighting. Jared was coming home grumpy, tired of the antics and constantly trying to survive one more day. I saw friends and family drifting away, not wanting to have us over because they feared that Lauren would have a meltdown. Our family became five people living their own lives. That stung, but I didn't know how to fix it. I started thinking about how life would look if Lauren were away. I couldn't believe I was even entertaining this idea. How does a mother think about sending her child away?

At Child's Place, we were assigned a counselor named Steph. She was young, but nice, caring, and informative. We had family therapy once a week. "How do the kids here at Child's Place get to live here?" I asked.

"Well," Steph said, looking puzzled, "some of them are here because they don't have parents or they are in the middle of some legal issue. Some are unable to go home because of behaviors, so they go to school here and then stay and board. Why are you asking?" she asked, her head tilted to the left.

"We were just wondering if Lauren would qualify to live here. Home has just been kinda tough." I started tearing up. "Lauren is struggling with friends. Nobody is available to hang out and the ones that are available are up to no good. We can't get her to do any chores or schoolwork, and there is constant bickering. Her temper is such that we can't leave her alone with her sisters. We can't ever go anywhere for fear she will have a meltdown in public. We're just at that point. I feel that this family dynamic is robbing our other two girls from the calm and organized home they deserve."

Steph crossed her legs. "Lauren would qualify to live here if she were younger. She is pretty much at the end of seventh grade. Unfortunately, she is too old to live here. Our age for kids is three to twelve. Lauren will be thirteen in September, right when school starts."

"Okay," I said, defeated. "I was just wondering."

"I'm sorry," Steph said. "I wish I could help."

"Yeah, me too." I followed Jared to the door.

CHAPTER 18

"WE NEED THIS VACATION," Jared said. "The kids will be fine. My parents and Kaelynn will be here 24-7." Kaelynn was somewhere between a babysitter and a nanny, and she had known the girls for about five years. She knew Lauren better than almost anyone.

"I know," I said. "Lauren is just so unpredictable."

I was excited to get away, and I loved the beach more than anything. We landed in Cancun and took a taxi to our hotel. It was sunny, hot, and very humid. I loved it. People were walking around outside, wearing shorts and flip-flops. When you live in the Midwest in the middle of winter, you forget what bare feet feel like. It was a very foreign feeling, taking off boots and replacing them with flip-flops—not that I was complaining.

We went to the beach every day and returned to the room at four to get ready for dinner. "The Wi-Fi is not excellent here," I said. "It might be tricky to Skype with the girls." I was ready, and Jared was still dressing. "I'll try to see if it works." A few seconds later the screen popped up. "Hi, guys," I said. "How's it going?" I could see my face in the camera; I looked a little red.

"Hi, Mom. We're good." They were all trying to get in the camera's line of sight.

"What are you guys doing tonight?"

"We are planning on going to Kaelynn's house. Her cousins are there, and we are going to have dinner and maybe play games."

"Awesome, that sounds great. Have fun! Talk to you tomorrow." I felt relieved that they had something planned. Now, I could go and enjoy the evening with Jared.

We walked across the street. I was always told not to go off the resort property in Mexico. I was very pleasantly surprised to see that, in this area at least, most people did go to the shops and restaurants outside the resort. I love looking at all the people on vacation. "Everyone has a different story," I said to Jared. "But some seem a little more interesting than others."

He looked at me and nodded.

"I'm beat," I said as we opened our door with the plastic key card. "I'm a little sunburned on my face and shoulders." When we entered the room, I immediately wanted to check my phone for missed calls. "Can you unlock the safe so I can look at my phone?" I went to sit on the balcony. I saw a missed call from Lauren's iPod. *That's funny,* I thought. *How did she do that? I can't keep up with the technology these kids use.* I pushed the button and redialed her iPod. I was connected, but Lauren looked mad. *Crap,* I thought. "What's wrong, Lauren?"

"Mom, I'm tired and I want to go home, but Kaelynn says I have to wait."

Right away I knew this wasn't going to be pretty. It was nine o'clock back home. Lauren was like a toddler. When she was tired and ready for bed, she had a window of time; if you missed the window, she would melt. "Lauren," I said, "where is Kaelynn?"

"She's playing cards with her cousins."

"Okay, go and give her the iPod. I want to talk to her." Lauren handed the iPod to Kaelynn. "Hey Kaelynn, when do you think you will be going home? Lauren is tired, and I don't want her to have a meltdown for you."

"We're planning on leaving pretty soon."

"Okay, thanks. Can you tell Lauren the plan? That will help her and her anxiety."

"Will do. Thanks," she said.

I walked back into the room. "That was Lauren," I said to Jared.

"Oh, what's going on now?" He seemed annoyed that I had looked at my phone.

I explained the situation. Jared didn't seem too concerned, but my stomach was churning. "I don't feel well," I said to Jared. *I knew being this far away from home wasn't a good idea.*

"Maybe it's the Mexican food," he said as he flipped through channels. Now I was annoyed too.

I took off my makeup and put on my pajamas.

"Kari," Jared said. I could tell he didn't want to tell me this. "Your phone is buzzing." I pushed the green button.

"Mom," Lauren said through tears.

"What the heck is going on?" I said.

"I'm tired, and I want to go home." It had been an hour since Kaelynn said that they would be "leaving soon." "Mom, can you come home?"

"No, Lauren, I'm sorry. I'm in Mexico until Sunday. Let me talk to Kaelynn again."

"Okay, but she is not going to leave." She handed the phone to Kaelynn.

"Hi," Kaelynn said.

"Kaelynn, I need you to load up the kids and take them home.

It's after ten."

"Okay, we're leaving."

I didn't want to sound annoyed, but I knew what was brewing. "Not in twenty minutes, I need you to leave now. Lauren is going to blow."

"Yeah, Kaelynn," I heard Lauren say.

"Lauren, don't talk to Kaelynn like that. You need to be respect-ful," I heard a woman say in the back. I motioned for Jared to come outside. He was not at all interested in the escapades going on at home.

"Don't touch me, bitch," I heard Lauren tell the woman.

I needed to call someone who could help me. "Kaelynn, I'm going to call my mom." I dialed my mom's cell number about ten times. *Seriously, this is the one time my mom doesn't have her phone with her?* I looked inside and saw Jared in bed with the covers pulled up to his chin. I dialed Lauren back, and Kaelynn answered. "Hey, is she any better?"

"Um . . . Lauren ran away."

Really, that wasn't surprising. I knew she was going to melt. "Do you have any idea where she might have gone? Why did she run away?" I had so many questions, and I was talking to an iPod.

"We were getting ready to leave and Lauren was in the car, and my mom and cousins were kinda mad at her, and she was yelling at them."

"Are you home now?"

"Yes," Kaelynn replied.

"Where is Megan?"

Megan took the iPod from Kaelynn. "Mom, I'm scared. They are so mean. They said they were going to call juvy. What is juvy?"

Holy shit, are you kidding me? I banged on the window to let Jared know I needed him. He sat up, and I motioned for him to come out.

"What?" He said, annoyed, as he slid the glass door open to the deck. He was not interested a bit. I tried to explain the situation. "What am I supposed to do about it?" he said. "I'm in Mexico." He walked back into the room, turned the light off, and got back into bed. I knew he was frustrated because we were on vacation and this crap followed us everywhere.

"Megan, you and Nikki go inside and get your pj's on. Please help Nikki brush her teeth and help her to bed. I'm going to call Grandma and Grandpa."

"Okay, Mom," she said.

I finally got my in-laws to answer, and I explained the situation.

"Okay, we are on our way over there now," Grandma Cee said. "Do you have any idea where Lauren might be?" My mom saw my calls and rushed over to our house, not knowing what was going on, and Grandma Cee brought my mom up to speed.

"No, I don't," I said. It was almost eleven. It was dark. I felt so helpless. Someone else was calling me. "Hang on a sec," I said to Grandma Cee. It was my neighbor Elizabeth. "Hello," I said, having no idea what I was going to hear.

"Mom!" Lauren was sobbing.

"Lauren, where are you? What happened?"

"They told me I was going to juvy. That's jail for kids, Mom! I don't want to go there. So I ran over to Elizabeth's."

"Okay, let me talk to her."

"Hi," Elizabeth said sleepily.

"I am so sorry," I said. "I'm in Mexico, and I don't know what's all going on. Can you send Lauren back to our house? Both sets of grandparents are there now." Elizabeth lived two houses down.

"No problem," Elizabeth said.

Lauren ran up to Grandma Jane and gave her a big hug. Kaelynn was upset. Grandma Cee was visiting with her. I was on the iPod, trying to listen.

Kaelynn was crying. "I didn't mean for any of this to happen," she said.

"We know, Kaelynn. We don't know what happened," Grandma Cee said.

"They were going to send me to juvy!" Lauren yelled.

"Okay, Lauren, you are okay now," Grandma Cee said.

"What's the plan?" I asked from the iPod.

"I think we'll take the girls now," Grandma Cee said to Kaelynn. "Lauren can be a handful."

Kaelynn was crying harder. "I'm so sorry. I didn't mean for any of this to happen," she sobbed. Grandma Jane gave Kaelynn a hug.

"I'll help with the girls too," Grandma Jane said as she held the iPod. Grandma Cee nodded.

"We know, Kaelynn. It will just be easier if we take the girls until Kari and Jared get home. Kaelynn, I will call you when I get home."

"Okay," she said with a heavy heart.

I walked into the room. It was after midnight now. I crawled into bed and rolled to my side, far away from Jared.

CHAPTER 19

LAUREN WAS DOING WELL in school at Child's Place, but evenings were tough. Our family dynamic was running like a worn bicycle tire; it got us from point A to point B, doing its job, but it was bumpy and uncomfortable.

I started looking online at summer camps for Lauren. I was thrilled to see there were camps for kids with emotional needs that lasted four to six weeks or longer. I called and inquired about a specific program. I filled out the application and spent time on the phone speaking to the owner, trying to decide if Lauren could handle the camp. "Lauren requires twenty-four hour supervision," I explained to the owner. "She doesn't read other people well at all. She assumes every word anyone says is a direct dig to her personally."

"Let me look into this, to see if this we would be a good fit for Lauren. I will get back to you," he said. So I waited.

About a week later, I got the call from the owner of the camp. "I'm not sure Lauren would be a great fit here at camp. I don't think we have the level of care she would need. I'll tear up your deposit. I'm sorry. I do hope you find something that will work for her."

"Okay," I said, and hung up. I sat at my computer and cried. I seemed to be crying a lot these days.

Summer was upon us and we loved being outside. I invited both sets of grandparents over for burgers. "Everything is almost ready," I said to the crowd on the deck. The home phone rang. "Hello? Mommy?" Lauren said, crying.

"Honey, what's wrong?"

"Mommy, I'm at the park, and some of the kids told me to call 911, so now the police are coming, and everyone ran away. I'm going to go to jail."

"Lauren, I will be right there." I hung up and turned to my mom, "I'm going up to the park. I'll be back in a few minutes."

"Is everything okay?" she asked, concerned.

I didn't want to get everyone worried. "Yeah, everything is fine." I smiled. "Jared, do you want to get the lemonade and bring the other salads out?"

Jared looked at me like, *What the hell is going on?* but knew he couldn't ask in front of everyone.

I jumped in my van. The park was at the elementary school, about four blocks from our house. I drove into the parking lot; it was empty, except for Lauren on her bike and Molly, the dog. "What happened?" I asked.

"There were these kids, and they told me that the people over there"—she pointed at the park in the distance—"they said were taking pictures of me. The kids said that it's illegal and that I should call 911. I didn't know what to do. They said they would wait, so I called 911, and they all ran away laughing. I don't want to go to jail." She cried harder.

"Lauren, you are not going to jail," I consoled her.

Just then one police car came into the parking lot and stopped near us. The officer got out of his car. Lauren was so scared that she was about to fall over. "Hello," he said kindly. "Did you call 911?"

I explained the situation. I told the officer that Lauren was high-functioning autistic and had some other special needs. "She knows to call the police for emergencies only." Lauren was crying.

"Don't worry, sweetheart," the policeman said to Lauren. "You're not in trouble. Can you tell me where the kids are that told you to call 911?"

"I don't know," she said. "I know them from my old school, but I don't know their names."

"Okay, well you go home with your mom and your dog. Nobody is in trouble." He talked to her a little about the police and how they help, and told her she shouldn't run away from the police.

I followed Lauren on her bike and took Molly in the backseat. It hit me then, with such force that it took my breath away, that I really couldn't ever let Lauren go off on her own. She was way too vulnerable. She could get into all kinds of trouble and wouldn't even know it.

We got home; I went to the porch and explained what had happened, and then said I was going to my room. I told Jared they could go ahead and eat without me. I closed and locked my bedroom door and sat on my bed. I took a clonazepam, put my head on the pillow, stared into space, and cried.

I was confused when I opened my eyes. I must have slept the whole night. I felt a little better after I woke up a bit. After Jared left for work, I sat down on the computer at the kitchen table and started looking for something. I really didn't know what I was looking for, but I knew we needed help and I was going to find it. This was all uncharted water for me. I felt Lauren was not getting the assistance she needed to succeed. I started looking for special-ed schools. There weren't many that would be helpful to Lauren. *Think. Boarding schools? Those would be great if she were able to go to school and function,* I thought. I typed in "boarding schools for kids that don't like school," thinking I would delete it and look again, but some schools popped up. *Therapeutic boarding schools?* There were schools that actually helped students who struggled emotionally. I sat there, perplexed. I looked further—"boarding schools for kids with emotional issues"? Bam! Pages of schools and programs came up. I clicked on a school. *Girls' program, DBT—what is that? One- to two-year program, what does that mean? What are family sessions, family weekends, level systems?* It was too much. I decided to call a school, just out of the blue. I printed off the school and the program so I could take notes.

"Daybreak Academy, this is Andrea. Can I help you?"

"Um, hi. My name is Kari, and I wondered if I could get some information."

"Yes, Kari, what questions do you have?"

I paused. "Ummm . . ." I was completely unprepared. "I guess *everything.* What is a therapeutic school, and how can you help my daughter?"

Andrea giggled. "Yes, of course, most people don't know how to start that conversation. This is new to everyone at some point. Usually, parents get to the point of looking up schools when they're overwhelmed with decisions and feel they have nowhere else to go. Tell me about your daughter."

"Her name is Lauren. She's thirteen. She's in seventh grade, technically, but she hasn't really been in school all that much. That's where we are struggling. Lauren has ADHD, anxiety, depression, a learning disability in math, and high-functioning autism."

"Oh, my, I'm sorry. That must be hard," Andrea said. "That is a full load, poor kid."

That was one of the first times I heard someone think about the diagnoses and express genuine concern about Lauren's feelings and how hard this must be for her. I think I had forgotten that it wasn't about me; Lauren was the one suffering. "So," I asked, "one thing I couldn't find was tuition. How does that work? Insurance?"

"Well, that is a great question. We're pretty middle-of-the-road with respect to other facilities. Our tuition is nine thousand dollars a month."

I started laughing. "Are you kidding? How do people pay for that? That's insane."

"Well, we do have a waiting list," Andrea said. "Sometimes grandparents or other relatives will help. Some insurances will pay, and other families take out a loan."

"Okay, well, it was nice talking to you." There was no way this was even going to be an option.

When I told Jared about the experience, I thought he would blow. But he seemed intrigued with the idea.

"Yeah, it's a lot of money, but can they help her? I mean, keep her in school and help her understand that what she is doing is hurting herself and our family?" He paused. "She needs help, and I can't help her." Jared was tearing up. "And apparently no one in this town can either. I'm not seeing very many resources for teens with mental illness."

So I called them back and got more information. They were full, which I couldn't believe, considering their prices, but they'd have a spot in a week or two. They had two different houses in the program Lauren would join. The houses were massive, and each had around thirty girls. The houses shared a school off-site, and there was counseling and care twenty-four hours a day. The girls were never without supervision. They moved through five different levels, and their level determined what privileges they could have. There was hiking, canyoning, swimming, cliff jumping, rock climbing, and camping. There was even a swimming pool and a cook who prepared all the meals.

I told them about Lauren's issues, and they seemed to think she would do well there. We would have to fill out an application and have medical records sent. Then they'd have a formal meeting to discuss if they thought Lauren would be a good fit.

"I went to the bank over my lunch break," Jared said. "We qualify for a line of credit that could cover the tuition. You may have to go back to work, though. This is going to get expensive."

"I know," I said. But right now my biggest concern was how I was going to approach this with Lauren.

After school, Lauren asked if we could go to the dog park.

"Yes, Lauren, we can. Get Molly ready."

But Lauren wanted to find someone to come and hang out with her. That meant that Lauren would call everyone she knew and beg them to come, bribing them with treats and rides. It was a two-hour process. But I always fell into the vortex of her plan. Maybe it was because I didn't want the fight, or because Lauren had no friends and I thought that this might be the one time she would succeed in making one. When it worked, I found myself getting upset because I was always entertaining everyone else's kids. No one ever reciprocated. Whether that was because they didn't want to, or they didn't have the money and time, or their kid didn't want to hang with Lauren, I had no idea.

This particular day, Lauren couldn't find anyone who wanted to come to the dog park. It was extremely painful to listen to. "Hi, this is Lauren. Gusso. Um, I was wondering if you wanted to go to the dog park with my mom and me. You can bring your dog too. We can go for ice cream. My mom can pick you up and bring you home. Okay. Oh, okay. Bye." I could see her deflate. "Mom, why doesn't anyone like me? I try so hard. I don't think anyone wants to be friends with me. I just want a friend." She sat quietly for a few minutes and then looked at me with teary eyes. "If I died, I could go to heaven, and Jesus would be my friend." She started crying. "I want to meet Jesus, Mom. Jesus will love me, he promised."

I started sobbing. *How could I answer that statement? Jesus wants you to live? Jesus doesn't want to meet you now, wait until you are old? What am I supposed to do?* "Meeting Jesus" was not in the parenting handbook.

I supposed this was as good a time as any. "Lauren, there's a school in Utah that helps teen girls with their emotions." Lauren looked interested. I grabbed the paperwork that I printed off. "Look, here it says they do school, but they also go on some amazing trips. They go camping, hiking, rock climbing, and cliff jumping." Lauren perked up. "It's in Utah, so you would have to live there. I think this school would give you an opportunity to make friends, and they could also help you with your feelings and emotions. Daddy and I just want you to go to school and be happy." I prepared myself for an argument.

"I want to go to the school." She said it almost emotionlessly.

"Oh, um, okay. I will call and set it up." I couldn't believe it was that easy. I was sure the wheels would fall off, as they always did. But I had no idea what to expect.

JARED AND I PROCESSED this situation differently. I think he saw her leaving as a business plan—"Why wouldn't she go? That's the best plan, right?"

I, on the other hand, was crying, overeating, oversleeping, completely hopeless—a hot mess. My mom was even worse. She felt all the feelings I felt for Lauren, but she also felt sad because I was *her* daughter and I was struggling, and she couldn't fix it for me. My mom started crying and didn't stop for about a month.

"How many suitcases am I bringing?" Lauren asked.

"Well," I said, sitting down and thinking about it, "I think you will need one for your linens, towels, and pillows, then another one for clothes: shorts, pants, sweatshirts, jackets, T-shirts, swimsuit, underwear, bras, socks, and shoes. We need to bring a bag with your toiletries, and you'll want to pack Snuggles." Snuggles was the bear Lauren had received from my mom on her first admission to the psych hospital at age nine. She had slept with it ever since. I pulled their list from my pocket. "They said you could bring photos but no frames with glass, and shoes to wear outside. Also no hoodies or sweatshirts, or pants or shorts with strings." *Huh, these are very bizarre rules.* "No makeup, no jewelry, no perfume, no razors, and no nail clippers."

I didn't sleep well the night before we left. I even took two clonazepam pills. I was so anxious that I could feel my heartbeat in my head. Lauren, on the other hand, was cool as a cucumber. She was ready to go, excited for this new adventure. I didn't know if I should be happy that she was taking this so well or terrified because she had no idea what was about to go down. I needed her to be carefree for the next few days while we flew into Las Vegas and made our way to Utah. I didn't think I could take her and then leave her if she were fighting me or crying and not wanting to go. *I guess ignorance is bliss,* I thought. *And at this point, I'll take ignorance.*

"I WANT TO SIT by the window." Lauren was so excited to go to a new school. She wanted a chance to start over.

"Lauren, you need to calm down a little. Where are your Beats?"

She pulled them out of her bag.

"Where is your iPad?"

She pulled the tablet out too.

"Okay, why don't you watch one of your movies or listen to music?"

"Okay, Mommy," she said.

I could hear the bass of the music in her headphones. "Her music is so loud," I said to Jared. But I'd learned not to bother Lauren if she was listening to music, happy, and quiet.

The outer glass doors of the airport slid open and we walked outside. I felt like I had landed on Mars and forgotten to put on my spacesuit. The dry heat sucked all the air and moisture out of me. We boarded a shuttle, which was blasting frigid air.

Vegas had the tourist system down to a tee. Landing, getting our luggage, taking a shuttle, and renting a car took less than an hour. We drove up to the big hotel with bright lights, and there were bellmen outside ready to help us with the car.

We walked into the lobby, where the lights were bright and blinking in a multitude of colors. Waitresses walked by, wearing almost nothing and selling drinks. There was a clinking of coins and slot machines, and, of course, the *ding ding ding* of a winner.

"Give me the key." Lauren ran to the room and opened it. Twenty feet behind her, I could hear her say, "Oh my gosh, this is awesome." We had a two-bedroom suite that overlooked the pool. Off in the distance was a Ferris wheel that looked to be at least fifteen stories high.

We left to go shopping on the Strip. We passed a man sitting on the ground with a sign. Lauren looked at me. I kept walking. "Please don't make a big deal of this," I whispered to myself.

"Mom! Stop! Don't you care?"

"Lauren," I paused. This wasn't a situation we had to deal with back home. I thought of stories I'd heard of con artists posing as homeless people and hurting the people that tried to help them. I kept walking.

"No, Mom, why don't you want to help?" she said loud enough for people to hear.

"Lauren," Jared said, "let's go back to the hotel, and we can talk about this."

"Do you know that Jesus would help him? Mom, you are acting rude."

I was getting nervous now. The last thing I needed was Lauren having a meltdown on the strip in Vegas. I gave her five dollars, and she handed it to the man.

"Mom, we should get him food. He could come to the hotel with us, right? We have room, Mom, please."

How could I say, *No Lauren we are just going to ignore him and go back to our warm, cozy hotel room after our super-large meal. Is this a lesson for her or me?* "Lauren, you gave him the money. There are places he can go to get help, shelter, and food. We just can't do anything right now."

She stomped away. All I could do was follow her and hope that we got to the hotel room before any extreme emotions erupt. In the elevator, going up to floor twenty-three, she said "Mom, some people need help. We were given money so we could help others."

"Lauren this is a very complicated issue. You're right, and we should help. Daddy and I give money and donate clothes to charity three or four times a year. Sometimes you just don't know who you are giving the money to." I wanted to mention the kind of habit we could be feeding, but I didn't want to open that can of worms.

As I was putting on my pajamas, I said to Jared, "I am worried about Lauren in the big world."

"What do you mean?"

"I'm afraid that Lauren would give everything she had to help someone, and that is very Christian of her, but people are mean and vindictive. Someone is going to take advantage of her, and she is going to get hurt. She doesn't seem to have any concept of where the money comes from or what to do with it, and she sees everyone like a best friend." I sat on Lauren's bed, rubbing her back as she was sleeping. How was I going to leave her alone? She was only thirteen. Leaving her in Utah was going to rock her world.

THE SUN FOUGHT TO shine through the window between the drapes that were trying to keep the light out. Lauren bolted out of bed. "We all get to go to Daybreak Academy today, right, Mom? Can we swim before we go? Where is breakfast? How far is the drive?"

"Lauren, calm down, please. We can't swim because we need to go to Daybreak, and we'll get breakfast on our way out. It's about a two-hour drive to St. George, where our hotel is. We'll see Daybreak Academy, tour the area, and have dinner. Then we'll take you back to Daybreak Academy Monday morning and say goodbye."

I didn't know if it had hit her yet. Daybreak Academy was a therapeutic boarding school for girls twelve to seventeen. The therapeutic part of that was twenty-four hour therapy, care, and supervision. The girls who attended Daybreak Academy were girls with moderate to severe emotional dysregulation. Some were suicidal or severely depressed; some had abandonment issues, bulimia, anorexia, or oppositional defiant disorder; and some had been raped, become addicted to drugs, or prostituted themselves. They were a very diverse group. That was why it worked so well—they fed off each other, but learned from each other too.

"Okay, Mom," Lauren said.

The drive through Nevada, Arizona, and Utah was beautiful. Red dirt, mountains, desert plants, dust devils—everything was so different from the Midwest. The city of St. George sprang up with a huge welcome as we came up and out of the canyon. It was a nice, small city, not huge with skyscrapers and bumper-to-bumper traffic. Just a nice-size town. All the major stores, restaurants, and entertainment we could want. Our hotel was right at the end of St. George as you entered the small town of Hurricane. The people there pronounced it "Hurkin."

As we parked and unpacked, Lauren went looking for geckos and other small creatures. "Lauren, don't go too far on the path by yourself," I called to her. Near the hotel, there was a walking path that went through a park and kept going through the town, probably for miles.

"Mom, I got one. He's so little," Lauren said.

"Lauren, you probably shouldn't be picking up animals until we know what is poisonous and what is not."

"Mom, this is a gecko, and it won't harm you." She rattled off facts about geckos and other desert creatures.

"Jared, why don't you go with her and help her find animals," I said. "I'll get organized and meet you back here, and then we can go to dinner. Ask her what she is hungry for."

As we waited in lobby of the restaurant, I said, "Lauren, sit. The wait is not that long."

"Mom"—Lauren was nearly hyperventilating—"I can't sit. I can't eat."

"Okay, okay," I said. "Let's get it to go, then."

I went to the bathroom, and when I came back she was gone. "Where is Lauren?"

"She's outside," Jared said. When it was time to order, he went outside and then came back with a puzzled face. "She's not out there."

I got up and ran outside. "Lauren?" I yelled.

Jared went around back to see if she was there. "Kari!" he yelled. "She's down the road." He ran back to the car, and we drove about three blocks to where Lauren was walking.

"Lauren, what are you doing?" I asked.

"I'm going back to the hotel," she said matter-of-factly.

"Lauren, we didn't know where you were. Get in the car, and we'll go back to the hotel."

"Okay, Mom." She got in the backseat and looked out the window.

"Lauren, are you hungry at all?" I asked her.

"Not really," Lauren answered. I wondered if she was starting to see the reality of what was happening.

CHAPTER 20

"It's six in the morning, Lauren. What are you doing?"

"I'm going swimming."

"Lauren, it's way too early. Wait for Dad."

Jared rolled over and looked at me with an annoyed face. "I guess I'm going to the pool," he said, groaning and getting out of bed.

"There's coffee in the lobby," I said.

Lauren was hopping around like a black lab pup. "Come on, Dad, hurry."

"Yep, yep, I'm coming," he said, yawning. I fell back on my pillow.

When they came back from swimming and eating breakfast, it was time to get organized. "Okay, should we get going?" I said.

"I'll be ready in a bit," Jared said from the bathroom.

Lauren was already getting dressed in the room. "Mom, I'm going to go down and look for geckos."

"Lauren, please wait for me, and grab your suitcase and pillow on the way to the car." I called to Jared through the bathroom door. "Lauren and I are going down to the car."

"Okay," Jared said, over the noise of the shower.

"I'm going to miss going on these little nature hikes with you, Lauren."

"It's okay, Mom. Don't be sad. You're not going to cry today, are you? If you start to cry, then I'll be sad when you leave. Please don't cry," she begged.

"Okay, Lauren, I will not tear up. I promise." She ran ahead into the bushes. I stood there and smiled. She was so carefree, young, and naive. My throat started to get a little tight, the feeling I always got before I cried. *How am I going to get through this?* I thought. *I'm not this strong.* I just wanted to run down the path and not stop until I got home.

Jared was ready and standing next to the car when we came back from our walk. Lauren had caught a few critters, but thankfully she'd let them go. I plugged Daybreak Academy into my GPS. "It's about ten miles east. Just go up there and take a right and you can merge onto the highway," I explained to Jared.

The next twenty minutes were the most agonizing. We were driving into unknown territory, and I was scared to death. As the car kept moving forward, I kept thinking—*We can turn around. We're doing this voluntarily. What if this is the worst decision? Sending her away is the worst decision. We need to go home. Why does the car keep moving forward?* I wanted to throw up. We were leaving Lauren here without looking at the facility first. *Who does that? What am I doing? What kind of a mom am I?* We drove into the little town of "Hurkin," and I prayed that this place wasn't a total hole. What if it was a run-down home for misbehaving girls?

"Turn left in four hundred feet," Siri said in her monotone voice. Up ahead was a huge, lovely, well-kept house. There was a privacy fence blocking off the view of the backyard and a pretty, oversized wood door. It was open, so we walked in. We entered a public lobby, complete with a water cooler, couch, chairs, and information table. Photos of students rock climbing and swimming hung on the walls. The floor was tile, with a large area rug. Nobody was there, but we were early. I could not hold Lauren off much longer.

I knocked on one of the doors. It was locked, but I could hear people on the other side. There was a beep, and the door opened. "Hi," I said. "Um, this is Lauren, and we're enrolling her today."

A nice woman who looked to be about twenty-five led us into the house and through a door that locked behind us. There was a foyer, and to the left a hallway that led to a great room. Straight ahead was an eating area, then the kitchen and another large eating area. Off the kitchen were a bathroom and a set of stairs that went down to one bedroom. We walked into the great room, where they had a large, L-shaped couch, a rug, a TV, big windows, and more pictures of girls doing activities. A public restroom was on one side, and a broad stairway off to the right led to the second story. The upstairs had a large bathroom, with five showers, four toilet stalls, and four sinks. There were five large bedrooms and another large dayroom.

There were three or four beds in each room, and each girl had a closet cubby. Their toiletries were locked up along with their laundry supplies. There was a set schedule for laundry and for showering. The house was clean, organized, and well-mannered.

"Lauren?" came a voice behind us. "Hi, I'm Shirley."

I shook her hand. "Hi, this is Lauren." I looked at Lauren and stumbled on my words. "I'm Kari, and this is Jared." Everything looked great, but I was still nervous.

"Welcome to Daybreak. Did you have a nice flight?" We walked into the office, exchanging small talk. "We're excited you're here, Lauren. I'm going to get some information from your parents. You can go hang out with the girls, and I'll bring you back to your mom and dad when we're finished."

Lauren looked at me. "Don't leave," she said.

"I won't go without saying goodbye," I promised.

Jared and I sat on the couch. "We'll get some paperwork done," said Shirley. "And then Jake will be in shortly to say hi. He's the head therapist at Juniper." Juniper was the name of this group of girls.

We took about an hour finishing up the paperwork and meeting everyone. We had some laughs and also some tears. I was very nervous to say goodbye. I wanted to run away, not deal with it. Lauren came into the office. She was timid; I could tell that she was starting to understand that I was going to be leaving. In the orientation meeting we'd just had, they had mentioned that it would be at least two weeks until they let Lauren call us.

"Mom, I'm going to miss you."

I hugged Lauren, holding onto her for as long as I could. I just wanted the little girl, the toddler, with the big smile and great big ideas. I want to take her home and try again. I wanted a do-over.

"Okay, Dad and I are going to go. We will talk to you as soon as they let us." I didn't understand why parents couldn't talk to their kids, the kids who were struggling and needed the most love and support.

"Bye, Mom. I love you so much."

"Be good, try your best, and you'll do well," I said as I looked her in the eye. "You got this."

Jared leaned in and gave Lauren a hug. "Bye, honey. I love you."

We walked out the door. I kept waving and blew her a kiss. I opened the car door, got in, and turned on the air—I felt like I couldn't breathe. I waved goodbye like Lauren did when she was eighteen months old. She would wave with her palm facing her, her little hand going back and forth, backwards. I missed that baby.

All the hope and plans we had for her, her dreams, aspirations, what were they?

We drove down the highway in the opposite direction of our baby.

CHAPTER 21

To HELP PAY FOR Lauren's school, I started working full-time as an RN. My schedule was flexible, so I could take off time when I needed to for Lauren and the other girls. With flights, hotels, car rentals, food, gas, and insane tuition, we were very concerned about money. Little did I know, after Lauren's stay at Daybreak we would have spent over $150,000.

In November there was a quarterly parents' weekend, which was the first time Jared and I went back out to Utah. Our flight to Las Vegas got delayed, and we arrived at two in the morning. We got to the hotel by three, and we had to leave for Utah at four o'clock to make sure we arrived by seven thirty. The lobby of our hotel looked like it was three in the afternoon, not the morning; people were everywhere, doing everything. There seemed to be natural light from somewhere, but no clocks anywhere. We didn't even bother going to the room, although we did pay for it. We went to an all-night buffet and grabbed a bite, drank coffee, and stared at each other as we ate.

"Where do we go?" I asked when we got to Daybreak.

"The big wooden door is open; let's start there," Jared said like a smartass. We walked into the lobby; there were snacks, water, and staff waiting to welcome us.

I heard Lauren's voice. "Mommy!" She barreled into me, almost tackling me to the ground. "Mommy, I missed you so much. I'm so happy you are here."

"Hi, Lauren," I said as I gave her a giant hug. Other parents were doing the same with their daughters. I couldn't help but look around and think, *All these kids and parents have been down a similar road as we have.* I wondered what their stories were.

"Come and see my room," Lauren said, and took my hand and led us upstairs. "This is my bed," she said as she plopped down. The other girls were also in the room with their families.

"Hi, I'm Amalia," I heard another mom say. "I'm Jen's mom."

It took me a second to realize she was talking to me. "Hi, I'm Kari, and this is Jared. I guess Lauren and Jen have become pretty good friends."

"That's what I hear." Amalia and I talked for a bit. We had a lot in common. We were both nurses, had other children, and had a challenging teen who had led us to Daybreak. I met a few other parents. Everyone's stories were a bit different, but we were spot-on identical as far as family dynamics.

We were handed a folder with the weekend's itinerary. We had two full days of activities starting with group therapy, then art therapy, and finally recreational therapy. Lunch was here at the house, and tonight we had a movie night with dinner. Tomorrow we went to the great outdoors for hiking and caving.

"Let's get a seat for the group therapy," Lauren said, and she ran to the meeting room and jumped on the couch.

"Can anyone tell me a time they were scared?" Sal, the counselor, asked.

Lauren blurted out, "I'm scared when I'm mad."

"Okay, what makes you angry?"

"Stuff," Lauren said.

Another girl raised her hand. "Yes, Missy?"

"I'm scared when I'm out of control, and I feel—"

"Me too," Lauren said, interrupting. She stood up. "And I get mad, right, Mom?"

Missy shot back, "Lauren, don't interrupt me."

I looked at Lauren. "Missy was talking," I said. "Let her finish."

"Okay. Sorry, Missy," Lauren said quietly.

Our next session was individual therapy. "Is Lauren always this hyper, interrupting people?" I asked Sal, the counselor.

"That is something we are working on. We'll get through it," he said.

"It seems as if other girls are annoyed by her immaturity."

"Yeah, that is probably true," he said, "but there are always going to be older and younger girls to contend with here, and it's good that they are learning patience and compassion."

"Okay, if you say so." I felt terrible for the girls, but more so for Lauren; she needed to learn some social skills.

Lauren started telling us about her days so far at Daybreak. "When I first got here, I cried myself to sleep for about two weeks. I hate crying myself to sleep. I had to be on safety for a week. I couldn't go outside, and I had to be with the staff all the time. They had to stand outside of the stalls when I went to the bathroom, and it was so embarrassing 'cause they could hear everything. We can't shave, so my armpits and legs are going to get hairy. We have groups every day and school every day. I hate school, and I don't want to stay in school. I do 'cause I know I have to. We ride in the white ratchet residential van to school." She laughed. "We make fun of the van. We play good music though. There are off-campus outings that you have to earn. Girls go hiking, swimming, cliff jumping, biking, or bowling, or go to a movie. It's enjoyable if you get to go. We can only eat the meals that they give us. I get so hungry, Mom. I even got in trouble for taking food when the kitchen was closed. Overall, it's okay. I'm making friends, and being outside is fun 'cause I have people to hang out or play basketball with." She looked at Sal.

"Well, it's about time for lunch," Sal said.

I was hungry. Being up all night threw my body off, and I was exhausted. I got in line, got my lunch, and then sat down at one of the picnic tables in the eating area to eat my chicken salad. There were also croissants, fruit salad, and cookies. It felt good to sit and decompress for a moment.

Outside, waiting to start the next activity, I saw Amalia in the shade. I sat down on the grass. "Hi, Amalia. How are you doing? How is Jen doing with all this?" I asked.

Amalia was from Dallas, and she had a solid Southern accent. "Jen is okay," she said. "It's hard for her to be here alone. And it's stressful, with the cost and everything." Amalia was a single mom with another little girl at home. "I'm working as much as I can, like twenty hours of overtime a week, just to cover this tuition. We are living with my sister, and she helps with my other kiddo." I was in total awe of her. She was amazing, I didn't think I could do what she was doing. I had great admiration for how she was handling this situation. "I go to Africa every year for a few weeks, and we volunteer at an orphanage."

Just then Lauren and Jared came over with big scrolls of white paper. "I want to go to Africa," Lauren said as she overheard our conversation.

"Jen came with last year," Amalia said. "She loved it and did well."

"That is so awesome," I said. "I would love to go too someday."

"Me too," Lauren said. "Can we go, Mom? Please? Hey, Mom, if I get straight A's, can we go to Africa?"

Sadly, I thought, *I don't think Lauren is capable of getting straight A's. It's a safe bet.* "Sure Lauren, if you get straight A's, I will take you to Africa."

"Yippie!" she said.

Jared gave me his *seriously?* look.

For our next activity, we needed to trace Lauren on a big piece of paper. Then we would write positive things about her. "Lie still, Lauren; Dad is trying to trace you." All the girls were giggling as they were traced. It was windy, so I went and collected a few rocks to hold the edges down. I put a few words on paper, and then explained them. "Lauren, you are smart, funny, and great with animals, and you want to help people." I kept going. Then Jared went, and then Lauren listed things about herself.

"That was a fun project," I said to Jared. Lauren was already running around with Jen and some other girls. I was so thrilled that she was making friends. She had never had real friends before. Plus, Daybreak Academy was getting her to go to school, stay in school, and do schoolwork. *She's going to be okay,* I thought.

We went to dinner with some of the other girls and their families; we ate at a Japanese grill, where they cooked right in front of us. Everyone was laughing and having a good time. Lauren and some of the other girls got permission to spend the night with parents in the hotel, as they were trustworthy. I was so tired from going twenty-four hours with no sleep. I was pretty much a zombie getting in the elevator, going to the room, and getting into my pajamas. I lay down, closed my eyes, and was out.

"Mom, you snore. You snored all night. I heard you snore the whole night." Lauren was taunting me.

"What? Me, I snore?" I asked. "I didn't hear me."

"Really, Mom. That's because you were sleeping."

Jared was laughing. "Do I snore?" I asked him.

"I didn't hear you," he said wisely. "Let's get breakfast; it's on the main floor. We're going hiking today, so eat up. I don't know when lunch will be."

We were to meet at the pavilion inside the park at Zion. The mountains and hills were bright and colorful, and the day was beautiful and warm. "There everyone is," Lauren said, and ran ahead.

The lead started walking, and all twenty of us followed. Amalia was walking alone. "Hey, wait up," I said.

She smiled. "How did you guys do last night?" she asked me.

"Okay. I was so tired that I don't remember too much. I snore, evidently." I looked at Lauren.

"She does! I heard it all night," Lauren teased.

"How long is this hike?" I asked.

"It's about two miles. It's really cool," Lauren said. "The dirt path will end, and then you have a rock path. A little farther, you walk over rocks; then you get to a little lake that is hidden in the mountain."

We continued walking. The path got smaller, and then we started climbing. We didn't have a lot of mountains to hike in South Dakota, and I was stumbling over rocks and trying to look like I was in shape. *It's beautiful, but I'm going to break a hip*, I thought. As I was thinking of turning around, we rounded a corner and there was a tiny path. One by one, we shimmied through the opening.

I jumped down onto the dirt. It was about twenty degrees cooler than it was above, and damp. There was a small body of water— clean and cold, but small, like a pond. There was a little waterfall that fed the body of water and kept it slowly churning. I couldn't imagine that a place like this really existed. We sat there for about half an hour, just relaxing and enjoying the scenery and the people.

Our group started moving out, and we followed back down the rocks, trying not to break a bone. We walked until we found the broad dirt path.

I was sad we had to say goodbye today. I really did enjoy meeting the staff and all the other parents. I felt assured that we had made the right decision for Lauren.

The parent weekends were about every three months, and they were always different. The same parents were there each time until their daughter graduated the program. Then there were new parents trying to figure it out. On all the following parent weekends, we brought our other girls along for the cliff jumping, rock climbing, biking, hiking, touring local shops, and eating at excellent little restaurants. I cherish those memories now.

As Lauren moved up in her levels, she got to do more and more—activities she never would have done in South Dakota. When she first arrived, she was on "safety" and level one. She had to stay within arms' reach (safety) and eyesight (level one), and there were outings that she couldn't go on. In levels two and three, there were more privileges: makeup, social calls, and better outings. The last levels were four and five—those were like being a senior. There was a designated bedroom for levels four and five, and level fives got to go off campus on their own, maybe for a walk or to a coffee shop with another five. They also got to use cell phones and the internet.

Lauren worked very hard, and after about thirteen months of being at Daybreak she was finally a level five. She was on the pathway to coming home. We had plans in place for school, all our ducks in a row.

Lauren did great with supervision and a schedule, but being a level five was tough for her. She was fourteen years old and didn't do well with freedom and choices. She started to surf the internet, getting bad ideas and falling back into old habits. She went off campus to get ramen noodles, pop, and candy. These were the only foods she would eat. The counselors were ready for her to graduate from treatment. She was learning to "work" the program. Was it possible for a teen to get too much therapy? That was the place they thought Lauren was at—"therapied out"

We were thrilled when Lauren was discharged and was able to come back to South Dakota. Now the hard work would begin, as she was now in the real world. I hoped she could do it; I hoped *we* could do it.

CHAPTER 22

It took a few weeks for us all to get used to each other again. It was May, and school was just getting out for the summer. I had no idea how I was going to entertain Lauren until school started in the fall. Megan and Nikki had established friends—at least a few people to choose from. Lauren made friends with the three-year-old identical twins that lived next door. They loved Lauren, and they would follow her anywhere, mostly to catch frogs or jump on the trampoline.

Krystal wanted to meet at the high school to give Jared and me a tour, and she wanted Lauren there also. Lauren's anxiety could get the best of her, and she didn't function well when she was stressed or anxious. I just didn't want to get phone calls every day like I did when she was in junior high.

Libby, who was going to be one of Lauren's teachers that fall, offered to come and do some schoolwork with Lauren. "Mom, I don't want to read my stupid book with Libby," Lauren said, huffing. "I don't want to do school." Lauren stomped to her room. I stood in the kitchen and rolled my eyes. Libby and Lauren worked together twice a week for a month and a half.

When school started, it seemed to be going okay for Lauren. At the beginning there were a few bumps. Lauren was in a separate classroom, with other students who had similar issues. She had an IEP set up, but I didn't think they really did much with it. But after a week, Lauren started to struggle. She was anxious, sad, mad, and frustrated. She was having a hard time with peers. She argued with the special ed teacher, Libby. I was concerned. *Why can't they use her IEP as a guide to help her? Why does there seem to be no one equipped to handle Lauren? Surely there are other kids that struggle— or maybe I'm being overcritical.*

Lauren was starting to refuse to go to school. I would call the school and let them know that either she wasn't coming or I would get her there eventually. Three weeks into the semester, Lauren had yet to finish an assignment or read a book. Mental health always trumped academics. We were stuck. I had multiple meetings with her teacher, counselors, and principal, but we couldn't figure out why we weren't getting anywhere with Lauren. Large public high schools were supposed to have the means and programs to support students with issues like Lauren, but I didn't fully understand what Lauren needed and what her rights were as a student.

"Okay, yes, I'll be there as soon as I can." I hung up the phone. I had to leave work and go to the school to get Lauren. She was in the office and refused to go back to class. Apparently she got into it with her teacher and was asked to leave.

"I'm sorry," Mindy, my coworker, said. "This must be so hard on you." I knew they were genuinely sorry, and I did appreciate their kind words and prayers, but I was frustrated that they really had no idea what I was experiencing. I was getting no help. They meant well, but I was in a bitter place.

I pulled up to the school, left the keys in the car, and went inside to claim my student in the principal's office. It was about ten o'clock, and staff were buzzing around the office. Phones were ringing and the printer was spitting out papers. Waiting for Lauren, I saw a family friend sitting in the nurses' station. "Hey, buddy, you sick?" I asked.

"Yeah, my mom is coming to get me."

"Oh good. Okay, rest up. Hope you feel better."

He smiled an "I'm gonna barf" smile. Lauren came out of the back room, and I took her bag and swung it over my shoulder.

The principal was standing next to Lauren. "So we should probably set up a meeting with Krystal. This clearly is not working."

"Lauren said that Libby was crying," I said. "Is that true?"

"Well, Libby got pretty upset, and she was overwhelmed," he said cautiously.

"Okay. Have Krystal call me." Another kid walked in with his big backpack. "Man, you are busy in the office. We'll go and let you get to these other kids."

"Flu must be going around." He smiled as he walked to his office.

In the car, my phone buzzed. I had a message that said the high school was on lockdown. I gasped.

"What?" Lauren said. "What happened?"

"It doesn't say." Just then, another text came through. "Shots were fired, and a student is in custody." Then it said not to come running to the school and instead gave parents a number they could call.

A few hours later, I found out that a student, the one with the backpack who'd entered the office as we were leaving, pulled out a gun and shot the principal in the arm. The principal was fine, and no one else was hurt physically. The family friend locked himself in the nurse's station and hid in a closet.

I sat in a chair in the family room, thinking about what could have happened if I hadn't been on time to pick up Lauren. Then I had a wave of panic. *What am I going to do with her now?* The only place Lauren had done well was Daybreak. *Maybe she needs that boarding school atmosphere.* I suddenly thought of Dr. Dillon; her son went to a Christian coed boarding school north of here.

Jared and I met with the principal and some teachers and decided that it could be a good fit for Lauren. It was only a two-hour drive from us, and they had a van that transported the students to town on Friday and back up to school on Monday. There was a fair number of students from our town.

Move-in day was snowy and cold. January in northern South Dakota is brutal. The temperatures can dip to sixty below with windchill. It can be downright dangerous to be outside. "Lauren, grab the door," I said as I walked in the dorm with a big box full of pillows and blankets.

"Hi," a sweet-looking girl said.

"Um, hi," I said.

"Can I help you carry boxes? My name is Cyndal. I've been here for two years, and my sister is going to graduate in May."

I nudged Lauren forward. "I'm going to continue grabbing boxes from the car. Lauren, why don't you and Cyndal start setting up your room?" They both looked excited. Lauren was a freshman and Cyndal was a sophomore. About thirty students were roaming about the dorm. Boys on the right and girls on the left. The students seemed nice and receptive to their new student.

As I drove away, I waved and she waved back. *Please, please make this work, Lauren,* I thought. *I hope you can do it.*

For two months, I made multiple trips to Big Hill Academy. We set up a tutor for Lauren to keep her on task, talked to teachers about ways to help Lauren academically, and sat down with the principal to brainstorm ways to help her emotionally. Little by little, I could tell they were getting frustrated with Lauren's outbursts. Lauren and Cyndal were getting along well; she seemed like a good influence for Lauren. I kept telling myself that, one of these days, things would click for her. "I don't know how long this will last," I said to Jared. "I have no idea what we will do after this, if Big Hill Academy doesn't work."

About half of the students stayed at the dorm for weekends, especially in the winter. Lauren begged to stay up at school for the weekend. I checked with the staff, and everyone seemed okay with her staying.

"Jared, Sal is online." We were utilizing Skype with our counselor, Sal, from Daybreak. We tried to have a conversation once a week if we could all make it work. He knew us and knew Lauren. I hated starting with a new counselor and then explaining our life story for the thousandth time. Sal knew how to work with us, and we were comfortable talking to him. Lauren was on speaker. "Hi, Lauren. How are you?" Sal asked.

"Um, well, I guess I'm okay," Lauren said. She sounded distracted.

Jared started to explain that Lauren was staying up at school for the first time ever.

"Oh, wow," Sal said. "Lauren, how is it going?" he asked.

"Well, I think you're going to be mad."

"Why would I be mad?" he said.

"Did something happen, Lauren?" I asked.

"I don't want to tell you." Lauren was acting shy. "You are going to be mad."

"Lauren Grace," Jared said. "Tell us what happened. *Now.*"

"Well, um, okay. So I sorta snuck out last night with another girl—it was her idea—and we went in some boy's car and drove around. Then the boy came into my dorm."

My jaw hit the floor. "What? Are you kidding me?" *What is happening?*

"See, I told you you'd be mad," Lauren said sadly.

I didn't even know where to begin. "How did you sneak out? The doors and windows have an alarm on them."

"We disarmed it, by cutting the screen."

I hit my head lightly on the counter. "Do these boys go to your school?"

"No."

"How did you meet them?" I asked, knowing exactly what she was going to say. Lauren didn't have a great history when it came to social media. When she had access, which was very limited, she found situations that I don't think I could find if I tried.

"Facebook," she said matter-of-factly.

I sighed. "So you are telling me that these two boys drove two hours in this cold weather to your school dorm so you and your friend could sneak out?"

"I guess."

"You guess?" Jared said loudly. "Lauren, pack your things. I'll be there in two hours. You're coming home, young lady."

"What? I don't get to stay here?"

Is she crazy? I thought. *Why is she not putting this together?*

"Nope," Jared said calmly. "Does your staff know?"

"I don't know," she said.

"Lauren, you are probably suspended," I said, "if not expelled."

"I'm sorry, Mom."

Sal sat quietly, probably wanting to disconnect himself from this unbelievable situation.

"Get ready. Dad will be there soon." I hung up the phone. "Don't say anything. I don't even want to talk about it," I said to Jared. He grabbed his keys and slammed the door. Megan and Nikki were watching TV and had heard the whole debacle. "Bye, Sal. I'll be in touch." I ended the Skype call.

We grounded Lauren to her bedroom for the duration of the weekend. Monday morning, we heard from the principal. They were expelling Lauren. "Based on all the issues we have experienced with Lauren these last few weeks, and because she put the other kids in danger by inviting unknown males into the dorm, we feel it's best if Lauren looks for another school. We don't feel we can help her here at Big Hill Academy."

"Okay. We'll be up there to gather her things." I sat, perplexed. *What are we going to do?*

Entering the dorm felt like the walk of shame. "Lauren, grab a box and start packing."

Lauren was in rare form. The house mom came to inform us of the charges from the broken screen. She was less than thrilled. As she was telling me all about how this wasn't a good choice, Lauren started in. "You're a bitch. You are so mean."

"Lauren," I said. "Please go to the car."

"No, Mom. She's being a bitch to you."

"Okay, we are leaving now," I said to the house mom. "I will send you a check."

I called Krystal first thing the next morning. She already had a new school lined up. It was an alternative school called the Education Center, and it had more staff and tools that could help Lauren succeed. We also started taking Lauren to a social skills class, along with 4H and our church's youth group, but none of those were going great. Jared or I needed to be with her all the time. Otherwise, things didn't go well. The kid had no social skills or filter and was defiant all the time.

Lauren started at the Education Center the following week. Many students were in trouble with the law, on drugs, runaways, or truant. Some had horrible home lives, while others had just made bad choices. Unfortunately, those students were mixed together with students who "just suffer from a mental illness." The kids were treated like criminals when they weren't able to handle a situation. Then they became anxious and out of sorts because of their disability and mood dysregulation. I was starting to realize that South Dakota did not have the proper programs to aid this population. *You wouldn't punish a diabetic for having a low blood sugar,* I thought. *So why are we punishing someone who is bipolar and having a manic episode when both illnesses have a chemical dysregulation component?* But I couldn't seem to get anyone to understand my concern.

After trying to make the Education Center work and not succeeding, we decided to send Lauren back to Daybreak. She did well the first time she was there; why shouldn't it be able to help her again?

CHAPTER 23

"Happy birthday, dear Brandon," we sang. "Happy birthday to you."

"I'm so glad y'all could come for Brandon's Southern birthday," Katie said in her drawl. "I'm sorry Lauren couldn't be here."

"How is she doing?" my cousin Dani asked as she put her son on a blanket to play with some toys.

"Lauren is okay. But going back there was tough on her. She had to start the program over, and she's not buying it. That makes the process that much harder." I knelt down to give the baby a toy.

"Who wants cake?" my brother-in-law Ries yelled from the kitchen doorway. The kids came running. It was a great day to be outside. I had always loved fall.

My phone rang, and I looked down at the number. It was a Utah area code, but I didn't recognize the number.

"Mom." Lauren was crying. "Mom, I ran away."

"Okay," I said. I instantly had a headache. "Where are you?"

"I'm at a house."

"What happened?" I motioned to Katie and Dani that this was an emergency and I needed their help.

"I was mad," Lauren said, "and then I went outside and just ran. I'm at a house."

"Whose house?"

"I don't know, a family."

"Near the school?"

"Yes, it's not too far," she answered.

"Lauren, I need to know the address."

"Okay." She handed the phone to the owner of the house.

"Hello," a man's voice said.

"Hi," I said. "I'm so sorry that Lauren is there. Is she okay?"

"Yes, she is, but she seems very scared. Do you want me to keep her until you get here?"

I didn't know how to respond. "I know Lauren is scared," I tried to explain. "But Daybreak is not a dangerous place; they are not hurting her. I need her to go back."

"I don't know if that's a good idea," he said.

"Can I have your address?" He reluctantly gave me his address. I motioned for Katie to come to the phone. "Okay, thanks. Can you put Lauren on the phone?"

"Hi, Mom."

"Hey, Lauren. I need you to talk to Katie for a few minutes." I gave the phone to Katie and pleaded with her to not lose the connection while I called the staff to let them know where she was.

I called Bill, the director of Daybreak. "Hi," I said. "Are you missing a kid?" I was trying to make light of the situation.

There was a long pause. "Um, yeah."

"This is Kari, Lauren's mom. Lauren called me. She ran to a house. I have the address where she is at."

"Oh, good," he said. "This happens from time to time at facilities

153

like Daybreak, but they frown upon losing kids. It doesn't look good."

I gave him the address. The staff was excellent at Daybreak. I had gotten to know them very well. They were very good with the girls, very knowledgeable and caring.

I took the phone back from Katie. "Lauren, the staff is coming to the house. I told them the address."

"I don't want to go, Mom. I want to come home."

"What's going on? Why do you want to come home so bad?"

"I miss you, and they're mean."

"What do you mean, they are mean?"

"I can't do what I want to do. They don't listen."

"Lauren," I said as calmly as I could, "I need you to go back to the house with staff. I don't know the people you are with. That's not safe. Stay on the phone with me until the staff gets there."

"Okay."

"Who is all there with you?" I asked.

"A mom, and a dad, and two kids. They are nice. Mom, I don't want to go."

"Seriously, Lauren, you can't stay there." I was getting irritated.

"Mom," Lauren whined. I could sense she was getting anxious. "They are going to be mad."

"Honey, you need to go with them. You know they are not going to hurt you. You just need to go back to the house with the other girls."

"Oh no," Lauren said. "Mom, the staff is here."

There was a long pause. I heard voices and chatter on the other end. My other line rang; it was a Utah number. "Hello?"

"Hey Kari, Bill here. So we have a problem. Lauren is hesitating to come out of the house, and the gentleman that lives in the house is not opening the door until we prove that she is in fact in our custody as a student here. So we're going to have to get legal documentation. We'll keep staff here in the yard. It shouldn't take too long."

"Okay." I didn't know what else to say, so I switched back to Lauren's line. "Lauren Grace, why are you not coming out of the house? You need to go with Bill. They're concerned about you. Have they ever hurt you?"

"No."

"Are you scared of them hurting you?"

"No," she said calmly.

"You just don't want to go back to the house?"

"Yes," Lauren said slowly.

"Okay, Lauren, this cannot turn into a legal battle. You need to tell the man that you know the staff at the door and you feel safe going with them."

"I would, but he said he isn't letting me go. He wants them to get the paper that says I go to school there."

I tried to explain the debacle to mom and my sister. Everyone was crowding around me, trying to see what was going on. I felt so overwhelmed and tired. "I'm sorry this is ruining Brandon's birthday party," I said as I covered the mouthpiece of the phone.

My other line called again. "Lauren, hang on," I said.

"Hi, Kari. We have what we need and we're headed back to get Lauren," Bill explained.

"Okay. I'm so sorry that you had to go through this. What happened? Why did she run away?"

"She had an argument with a staff member, and they took away her free time." I could hear him walking. "I'm heading to the door; I'll call you and let you know when we have her with us." I clicked back to Lauren. "Hey, the staff is at the door. Please go outside with them."

"Will I be able to talk to you again, Mom?"

"Yes, Lauren. I will speak to you when you get back to the house."
I hung up, sat down on the floor of my sister's room, and cried.

My phone rang again. "Hi, Kari. We have Lauren and we're
heading back to the house."

"Okay, good," I said. "What's the plan now?"

"We will have to talk with Lauren and get back to you. She will
be on safety for sure," he said.

"Well, I guess she needs to be safe." I knew Lauren was not going
to be happy; in addition to her needing to be within arm's reach
at all times, this meant she had no phone privileges either. I was
so frustrated that they took away Lauren's calls home as a punishment. I knew there was a reason, but I hated it all the same.

MEGAN WAS IN COMPETITIVE cheer, and we traveled nationally to
compete. She loved that it gave her Mom-and-Megan time. We
drove to Chicago with my best friend, Kristin, and her daughter
Ella, who was on Megan's cheer team.

"Put a movie on, girls; it's going to be a while," I said, looking at
them in the rearview mirror.

Nine hours, three movies, and four bathroom stops later, we
were almost there. "Are we driving to the Bean?" asked the girls.
We were about an hour away from Schaumburg, where the competition was. "Please, can we go to the city? I want to see the Willis
Tower too."

I was tired of driving, but this was the first time I'd been to
downtown Chicago. "Okay, let's go," I said.

"Turn here," Kristin said. As usual, I drove and she navigated.
"Merge onto the highway and go north."

My phone rang. It was Utah. "Crap. What are the laws here for
driving and cell phones?" I didn't know and didn't want to get

pulled over. I switched to speaker mode and placed the phone on my knee. Kristin had been through all the drama with me; she knew how stressful it was, all that we had been through with Lauren.

"Hi, Kari. This is Sal. We have a bit of a situation."

"Oh no. What happened?" I asked.

"You want to get off at exit 56," Kristin said.

"Lauren is okay. She was mad at school about having to do an assignment over. She was able to get out the doors and tried running again. We were able to stop her, but we had to tackle her in the parking lot."

"Here's the exit," Kristin said.

My face lost all color. I wanted to pull over, but we were entering downtown and it was difficult to stop. "Is she okay?" I asked.

"Right here!" Kristin said loudly. I swung a sharp right. "Do you want me to drive?"

"No, it's fine. Let's just get there."

"She's okay," Sal said. "Just shaken up. She is so strong, unfortunately; she managed to swing and hit Andrea. Andrea fell and hit her head and had to go to the hospital. She has a concussion."

"Oh my gosh, I'm so sorry. Is she going to be okay?"

"Yeah, she will just need to rest for a week or so."

"The parking garage is up here," Kristin said. "Right after that donut place."

"Tell her I'm so sorry," I said. "Do we need to come out there?"

"See the sign?" said Kristin. "Turn here. No—*here*." We started to laugh at my driving, but I was crumbling on the inside.

"Not at this point," Sal said.

"Tell Lauren we love her and that we'll have to discuss this the next time we talk to her." I parked the car. I took a deep breath. "Okay, where do we go to get to the Willis Tower?" I said, forcing an upbeat tone.

As we walked, I trailed behind and called home, blocking out all of the downtown sights.

"Hey, Nikki. How's it going? What are you and Daddy doing?"

"Nothing," she said, sounding bored.

"Can I talk to Daddy?"

"Okay. Bye, I love you," she said. I heard her hand him the phone. I could hear her blowing kisses.

"Hey," I said. "Daybreak staff called me." I proceeded to tell him about the incident with Lauren. I followed everyone into Willis Tower.

"Do you want to go up?" asked Megan.

"What?" I said to Jared. My mind was reeling.

"Mom, do you want to go up too?" I plugged my open ear with the palm of my hand.

I shook my head. "I'll wait for you guys at the exit," I mouthed. "Have fun." I handed Megan a twenty. She rolled her eyes.

"What's going on?" Jared said.

"The girls are going up Willis Tower. But it's just easier for me to stay here and talk on the phone. Everybody gets tired of hearing all about our issues."

"Well, keep me updated about Lauren and Megan. Nikki and I are fine; you don't have to worry about us."

"I love you. Bye," I said and pushed end.

I sat down against the wall. Kristin came and sat down. "You didn't go up?" I said to her.

"Nah, I've been up before. The girls will have fun; I told them we would be here when they came out the exit. How's Lauren? How are you?"

I started crying. I just wanted to go and hold my daughter. "I don't know who needs who more."

The girls made it to the exit. "That was so cool, Mom; it's like standing on air. Look at this cool picture. Ella and I did handstands; it was freaky."

"That looks fun." I tried to smile. Megan knew how I was feeling, and I hated that this took the spark of fun out of the day. We continued to the Bean, had some dinner, and piled into the car to find the hotel. Kristin decided that it might be a better idea if she drove. I didn't argue.

The next morning, lots and lots of cheerleaders, parents, and family piled into the venue. "Did you sleep okay last night?" Kristin asked.

"I did. I was so tired, and I took a clonazepam, so I crashed."

"Are you feeling better today?"

"I am." I smiled. I was getting good at faking. "There are so many people here; I forget how big these venues are." We met up with the team and the other parents. I had made some lifelong friends through cheer. We were together for nine months out of the year. We'd cheer for each cheerleader when they finally got that back handspring and cry for them if they messed up in a routine. We knew who was doing what skills and which kids were neck and neck for the next spot on the senior team. It was competitive, but we also remembered that these were kids and it should be for fun. We may even have had an occasional glass of wine at the bar together, telling stories and laughing. I loved these weekends, when I *usually* could relax and not stress about life.

"We'll meet at one forty-five for parent prayer. You guys are on your own until then," the coach said to the team. Everyone separated like marbles dropped on the floor. Some went to get coffee, others went to get food, but many of them were doing makeup and hair. It was quite the process to get ready for a competition. The uniform and makeup were only part of the ensemble. Cheer was all about the hair and bow. The bigger the better, a sparkly bow sitting about one inch from your hairline. After nine years, I had perfected cheer hair. It was a significant accomplishment.

"Let's go down to parent prayer," I said. "Gather all your stuff, Megan. Look around and make sure you don't forget something." I was so excited to see them perform. Then my phone rang. It was a Utah number.

"Kari?"

Damn, I thought. "Hi, Sal. What's up?"

"Lauren is fine."

"I hate when you start a conversation like that." I turned to Megan. "Follow me," I again mouthed to her. "We need to meet your team."

"There's a problem with the gentleman that was at the house that Lauren ran to the other day."

"Yeah?" *I really can't have this conversation right now.*

"Well, apparently he was standing outside and saw the whole incident when we had to restrain Lauren. He happened to video the whole thing. He was concerned for Lauren, which is good, but unfortunately, he went to the police with the video."

Megan tapped my arm. "Mom, we're starting."

I looked at her, and she knew. She walked to the circle alone.

"Kari?" My heart broke for Megan.

"Yeah, I'm here. I'm at a cheer competition with Megan." I wanted to get off the phone, but I needed to figure out what the next step was. "So what happens now?"

"Child protection were here and interviewed Lauren and us, and they are going to contact you."

Okay, great, I thought. *Now we'll have social services on our ass.* I knew how that worked. I'd worked with kiddos in the system, as a nurse. It was not fun.

Sal concluded. "Lauren is complaining of pain."

"Where? From what?"

"We're not sure. But she has a one-hundred-point-eight fever. The nurse is wondering if it's okay if we get her evaluated by urgent care. Her pain is in her lower abdomen."

Sigh. "Okay. Keep me posted."

"We will, Kari. Hang in there, and good luck with cheer."

I had missed parent prayer and the sendoff to compete. I didn't even get to say good luck and kiss Megan. I gathered my stuff; walked into the full, loud auditorium; and settled in to watch Megan and her team.

I texted Jared; I didn't have enough energy to talk on the phone right now. All around me, people were cheering and having fun. I wanted to find a dark room and take a nap. The girls ran their routine, and they were fantastic. Zero deductions. I smiled and cheered, but on the inside, I was rotting from anger and jealousy. I was so envious of all the parents, who didn't have to deal with this emotional roller coaster.

As usual, we went to dinner as a team. Everyone was chattering and giggling, drinking, eating, telling stories, and laughing until they cried.

I saw my phone light up. "Oh, I need to take this." I got up and walked outside where it was quiet.

"Hey Kari, this is Sal. They did an X-ray of Lauren's abdomen, and they're worried about her appendix. They are going to do a CT and some blood work."

"Okay." I thought for a minute. *How are we going to handle this? I wonder if she'll end up in surgery.* "I probably need to fly out there, right?"

"That might not be a bad idea."

"Okay, I'll look at flights." Because Jared didn't do well with hospitals and I was an RN, it made more sense for me to go to Utah and for Jared to fly to Chicago and bring Megan home in the van after the competition. She was going to be devastated. I looked at my phone, found a flight, then called Jared. "Hey, I just got a call from Daybreak. They're worried about Lauren's appendix. They're going to do more tests and a CT scan. Sal thought that one of us should go out there; he feels there is a good chance she'll end up in surgery."

"Okay. Look at flights and tell me what I need to do." Jared sounded deflated.

I looked at my phone and pulled up the internet. I started looking at flights, a car, and hotel rooms. I didn't know how long I'd be there.

Megan came outside looking for me. "Mom, do you want dessert? Everyone is ordering dessert."

"You go ahead. I, unfortunately, need to book a plane ticket for your dad to come here. I need to go to Utah. Lauren is sick."

Megan sadly turned around and walked inside. I saw her sit down; she was laughing and talking. She had the fake happy down pat, just like her mama.

Kristin volunteered to help Megan get ready for the second day of competition. Jared flew in early and was in Chicago by eight thirty in the morning. He took a cab to the hotel. I met up with him and said goodbye to Megan; I knew she was crushed. She smiled and went off with her friends.

Jared gave me a big hug. "Everything will be okay. Nikki is with Grandma and Grandpa. I have Megan. You go figure out what is going on with Lauren." He wiped my tears.

My cab was waiting outside. "I love you," I said and kissed him.

"Bye, sweets. Love you," he said back.

I got in the cab and waved to Megan, who was standing on

the curb, already in her uniform, watching me leave. "I love you, sweetie," I whispered. "I'm sorry."

I arrived at the gate a little early, so I decided to get a coffee. I sat and looked out the window at the other planes. The woman on the intercom started announcing the boarding procedures: Parents with children or anyone needing extra time boarding may board now. Veterans dressed in uniform may board now. Diamond, gold, and silver medallion members may board now, in that order. First class may board now. Anyone with preferred status may board now. Please walk on the special blue mat when you board. Then, finally: Anyone who purchased their ticket on a low-budget website with a maxed-out credit card may board now—but please avoid the blue mat.

When I landed, I saw I had another missed call from a Utah number. I called back.

"Hello, this is Paige," a younger woman answered.

"Hi, Paige. This is Kari—Lauren's mom. I just got to Vegas; I should be in Hurricane in about three hours. How is Lauren?"

"She's good; they kept her overnight to monitor her. They did the CT scan, and they think she has something called mesenteric adenitis."

I should know what that is, I thought. "What is that?"

"She has inflammation around her appendix. I guess this can be painful, and it mimics an appendicitis. They are going to put her on an antibiotic. She should feel better in a few days."

"Is she getting discharged today?" I asked. "Can I pick her up and take her to my hotel for the night and let her rest?"

"I will ask Sal," she said, unsure.

"I'll be there soon," I said, and hung up.

I stepped off the shuttle and rented a car. As I drove down the highway, past the hotels and lights, the Strip became a regular city.

I had never really thought about people living there. Anywhere you stood, you could see mountains in the backdrop. The redness of the dirt accentuated the bright blue sky. Such a different land-scape than the one I was used to in South Dakota.

Driving through the canyon, I lost cell service for about an hour. The radio was in and out. I kept pushing *search* until a station could be picked up. I didn't have any say in the kind of music I was going to get. I wasn't sure there were even radio stations out here. The dirt was getting redder as I got closer to Hurricane.

My phone dinged. I stopped for a pop at a gas station and was able to pull up the text. Megan's team did well, and they were waiting for the awards. I had another text from the staff, which said that Lauren was getting discharged and would be at the house. I got back in the car and drove the remaining half hour to Hurricane.

Lauren appeared okay, but she had lost some color on her face and looked tired. "Hey, sweetie," I said. "How are you?"

"Mommy!" Lauren said.

I gave her a big hug. "Sal said you could come to my hotel for the night to rest and I could bring you back in the morning."

"Okay, Mommy," Lauren said contentedly. We spent the evening watching TV and ordered room service for dinner. Lauren slept well; her pain was getting better. I could see she was homesick, but she held it together and we had no problems.

"Lauren, I have to fly home today," I told her, bracing for a meltdown.

"Mom, I don't want you to leave. I miss you. The staff here this time are different than last time, and they're meaner."

"Lauren, I don't know what it's like to be here, but we need to help you figure things out. You just need to get to know the new staff." At the house, the therapist, teachers, and main staff stayed the same, but there was a quick turnover of the evening and night staff. "You know the program; just do what you need to do." I didn't know what else to say to her. And now I had to leave her, my sick child, with strangers in a different state. Who does that?

CHAPTER 24

THE WEEKS FLEW BY. Lauren was feeling better, but still not thrilled to be out there. It was Megan's birthday, and we packed up the car and headed to the Mall of America for the weekend. Megan and her friends had saved their babysitting money, and they were going on a shopping spree. Nikki and her best friend Pyper were coming too; they wanted to see the American Girl Doll store and ride the roller coaster at Camp Snoopy. I looked at the girls in the rearview mirror—three teens all staring at their phones and giggling, and Nikki and Pyper playing on the iPad together. No one was fighting or yelling. All was well.

"Girls, we're in Mankato, about an hour from the mall. I'm going to stop at this McDonald's." Everyone piled out of the car and stretched. We ate a quick lunch, washed up, and were back in the car in about thirty minutes.

"Turn the music up, Mom," Megan said.

"Hold up," I said. "I need to figure out this road construction." The roads were confusing, and I was driving in circles. My phone

166

rang. "Megan, could you answer that?"

I was not paying a lot of attention to my phone; I was more concerned as to how to get to 169 North with the exit blocked. Megan handed me the phone without a word. "Hello," I said into my phone.

"Hi, Kari, this is Sal at Daybreak." My stomach fell. *Not now,* I thought. *I'm so tired of getting these calls. My phone is starting to give me PTSD.*

"Hi, Sal. Is everything okay?"

"Well . . ." He paused. "We have a problem. Lauren is really struggling. Last night she and about six other girls went ballistic and tried to take over the house. They were yelling, swearing, throwing furniture, pulling pictures off the wall—the staff didn't know what to do. They stood by the doors and blocked the girls from leaving as their peers were tearing up the house. They had to call the police. All but two girls settled down; we had to restrain Lauren. She's on safety now."

Megan knew something was wrong; I could see it when she looked at me. I started to tear up. I wanted to hold it together, but I was failing. I continued to hunt for the stupid exit to 169. I was driving in circles. I couldn't make my brain focus. "Is Lauren okay?" I asked, barely able to get the words out.

"She's safe." He paused. "Kari, Lauren needs more help than we can give."

"What do you mean?" I asked with a scratchy voice.

"We think she needs to be transferred to Salt Lake City, to the Children's Hospital, where they can evaluate her. We feel that there is much more going on here mentally."

I was still driving in circles. *Fuck this, how hard is it to make a stupid exit easy to see?* I pulled off the road and stopped in a parking lot. I was crying; the girls were quiet, but Megan was crying now too.

"How does this work?"

"We need to call the hospital and see if there is a bed. Then we'll go from there. It might be a day or two before we can get her admitted."

"So Lauren will be stuck in a room by herself for a few days?"

"Yes—well, she will have a staff member with her at all times," Sal said.

That certainly is not going to end well, I thought. I paused and took a deep breath. "How does she get to Salt Lake? Do Jared and I fly in and pick her up?"

"No, we do not feel that's a good idea. I don't think she will behave for you. I worry about her running."

All I could say was, "Okey dokey." *Seriously?* I thought. *She's my child. She isn't going to run.* "Should Jared and I fly to Salt Lake and wait for her to arrive? You think it will be today or tomorrow that she'll arrive?"

"That is probably a good idea," Sal said. "That is my best guess at this time; we will keep you updated, Kari. I'm sorry," he said, sounding concerned.

"Okay. I'll let you know what our plans are as soon as I know." I hung up.

"Mom, is Lauren okay?" Megan asked. Her friends had no clue what kind of home life Megan had been living. It wasn't their fault they didn't understand; they just didn't have a sibling with a mental illness.

"Girls, I need to call Jared. Give me a few minutes." They got out and sat on the grass a few yards from the car in the sun and fresh air. I called Jared and brought him up to speed on the situation.

"Seriously? Why?" Jared was upset.

"I don't know, Jared. They want us to go to Salt Lake, for the admission, and I don't want to do this alone."

"I understand. What should I do?" Jared asked. "Should I fly to Minneapolis?"

"I have the car; someone will need to drive it home." Kristin was not comfortable all by herself. The girls started playing tag. They were including Nikki and Pyper, and they all looked so happy.

"If Mom and Dad drove me up to Minneapolis, I could fly out with you. Mom could drive the van home, and Dad could drive their car home. What do you think?"

"Talk to them and let me know," I said, sniffling. "I'm in Mankato, and I'm going to keep driving so the girls at least have something to do today."

The drive to the mall had turned into Megan telling her friends all about Lauren and what it had been like growing up with a sister with a mental illness. *Maybe that's a good thing,* I thought. *She needs to start talking about her feelings and letting people know what is going on in her life. She is going to need support too.*

I pulled up to our hotel and checked in at the desk. I was in a daze, just trying to get from point A to point B. My gut ached for Lauren. I knew she needed to be kept safe, but as a mama bear, I wanted to rush in and comfort her. They'd had to restrain her; the image flashed through my brain. My fingers were tingly. I took a deep breath. The woman handed me the key, and I walked back to the car. Everyone was already out and had all the luggage in the big cart. "Okay, here's a key." I handed one to Megan. "We're in 409. I'm going to park, and I will meet you up there. Keep Nikki and Pyper close."

A call from Jared came as I was walking from the car to the front door. I sat on a bench in the entry area. It smelled like smoke. "What did your mom and dad say?" I asked.

"They're getting organized, and we'll get on the road as soon as we can. It will be six before we get there. Did you look at tickets?"

"Not yet. I was going to get the girls situated and then search. I will stop at the front desk and book another room for your mom and dad tonight; they can sleep in our room tomorrow night with the girls. The room has a pullout couch and another room with two sets of bunk beds. So there is plenty of room and privacy." *All this traveling—the hotels, car rentals, and plane tickets—is getting expensive.*

"Mom," Megan said as I walked in the room. There was a faint smell of chlorine. "Mom, we want to go swimming. Can we not do the mall today?"

"That is just fine," I reassured her. Nikki and Pyper were elated. "Go get your suits on." The girls scurried off like ants. I looked at the TV; the Disney channel was on. I wondered if other families had this much drama—for us, every day was some new crisis.

I hadn't realized that our "pool" was actually a waterpark. Nikki and Pyper's eyes were as big as saucers. No wonder the girls were so excited to swim. We found a table. "Girls, go play; I will be here if you need me. But if you go to a different pool, tell me, so I know where you are." They nodded and looked at each other, trying to decide on where to go first. I sat down and opened my computer.

Airplane tickets—*click*, two tickets bought. Hotel—*click*, two nights reserved. Rental car—*click*, two days booked. The total was almost two thousand dollars. I put my head on the table. It was almost a hundred degrees in here; I needed to go swim. I realized I didn't have my suit, and I couldn't leave our stuff alone. *Ugh.* I sat back, watched the kids, and ordered a pizza.

Jared, Grandma Cee, and Grandpa Ned arrived at the hotel and came to the pool. "There are still a few slices left," I said. "Don't worry about it being cold; it was kept plenty warm in here. Jared, can you stay here for a bit? I'm so hot. I'm going to the room to take a break."

Our alarm went off at four thirty the next morning, and Jared and I left for the airport. Walking to the gate, I had the feeling that I had been plucked right out of life and dropped in the garbage like an unwanted topping from a pizza. I was so tired of putting everything on hold because of a crisis.

As they started the boarding process, I swear I heard the worker say, "Super tired, out-of-money travelers that have nothing they need for this trip but have a child who is unwillingly being transferred to a mental health hospital because of severe emotional outbreaks may board now. But please avoid the blue priority mat as we scan your ticket."

I looked at Jared. "I might grab the blue priority mat and run." As we walked down the very narrow aisle, people fidgeting and trying and get out of the way, I couldn't help but look at all the families going somewhere. To grandma's house, to a vacation destination, or maybe to a cousin's wedding. I got so angry when I saw happy families. I smiled my fake "I'm awesome" smile, crawled into the overused airplane seat, and put my seat belt on. I wanted to disappear into another time, another world. I leaned my head on the airplane window, curled into a ball, and closed my eyes.

Salt Lake was new to me. From the plane window, I could see snowcapped mountains surrounding the city like a frame. "I missed a call from Daybreak," I told Jared, and listened to the message.

"Hi, this is Sal from Daybreak. Just wanted to update you on Lauren. Please call when you can." I struggled to get out of the seat while listening to voicemail.

"Make sure you have everything, your phone, purse, earbuds," Jared reminded me. "You keep forgetting things lately. I worry about you."

"I know. I worry about me too." I managed to crawl out of the seat and got off the plane. "Thank you," I said as we passed the cockpit.

CHAPTER 25

As soon as I was able to get decent service, I called Daybreak. "Hi, Sal. How is Lauren doing?"

"Lauren is fine. She is upset with the staff because she wants to be out of confinement."

"Confinement?" I said.

"Yes, she is in the safety room with staff at her side. She is just too unpredictable, with her running and all."

I nodded, not realizing that Sal couldn't see me. I started crying and handed the phone to Jared. We continued to walk towards the rental car area. Jared was very serious and nodding his head as he talked to Sal. I walked up to the desk and proceeded with the car rental. When I came back, Jared was sitting on the bench that was just outside the rental office. "What did Sal say?"

"Well, they are going to do their best to get her admitted, but it might be tough because it is Saturday. They will let us know when they know."

"I hope this admission process doesn't take forever," I said. "I would have gone to Hurricane if I knew that. I don't understand how this mental-health crap works, and I am very concerned."

"Let's get checked into the hotel and grab something to eat," Jared suggested. We ate and went back to the hotel room for the night.

"I wish I could just sit on her bed and rub her back. She loves it when I do that."

"Kari, I understand entirely what you are saying, but you forget about how much help she needs. She is unsafe. She won't go to or stay in any school, and I don't know what else to do. We can't leave her alone. You can't work. We need help."

I buried my head in my pillow and cried until I was asleep.

"WE NEED TO DISCUSS transportation options," said Sal.

"Come again?" I put Sal on speaker so that Jared could be in the conversation too.

"When we have situations like this, the child is transported by a professional service. They are trained to handle disruptive kids."

"Why can't we just get her?" Jared asked.

"We don't know how she will respond to you."

"Are you kidding? She's our child," I said. "I'm pretty sure we can handle her." Jared was shaking his head. "So what is this transportation thing?"

"It's a private company. You call and arrange the transport, and you pay them directly."

"Oh, crap. How much is that?"

Sal was silent for a few seconds. "It will run about two thousand dollars to get her to Salt Lake."

I sat down on the bed and stared out the window. I didn't know what emotion I had going on. I was blank. "So we just sit and wait for tomorrow?"

"Yes," Sal said.

I lay on the bed. Jared and I were alone with no kids for the first time in a while, but I just wanted to lie in bed and stare out the window all day.

Jared looked at me, trying to figure out if I had lost it. "I'm going to go for a walk," he said. The door closed, and once again I cried myself to sleep.

Jared tapped me on the shoulder. "Hon, I brought you a bowl of soup and a sandwich."

"What time is it?"

"Six thirty."

"Oh my gosh, I slept for six hours?"

"I came back and you were sleeping, so I left and got dinner."

I sat up. "That looks good. I'm hungry."

"I hope Lauren at least gets transported here tomorrow. I can't sit here for a week waiting," Jared said. "I need to get back to work."

"If we don't know anything by tomorrow, then I can stay, and you can go back to work and be with the girls. If she gets here tomorrow, we'll see her and make a plan then." Even though I had slept all day, I was still tired enough to go to bed for the night. "I feel like we left the other girls about a month ago," I said.

"Oh, I talked to Mom," Jared said. "They had a great time. They spent all day at the mall and were getting packed up and ready to drive back to Sioux Falls."

"Oh, good. I'm glad. Thanks for dinner," I said to Jared as I laid my head on his chest.

"Sure," he said, playing with my hair. I tried to stay awake through the movie we were watching, but I fell asleep.

THE SUN WAS SHINING through the little spaces the drapes had left open. It was very quiet. I walked to the window and looked out. The highway was packed, bumper to bumper. "Wow, these rooms are soundproof. I can't hear any of the traffic."

We went for coffee, and my cell phone rang just as we got back. "Hey, Sal," I said.

"Hi, Kari. How are you?"

"I've been better. What's the plan?"

"Well, there's a slight issue." *What could have possibly happened now?* "Lauren is fine," he said quickly. "But the hospital doesn't have any beds available for three days."

"No, that is not okay," I said. "She can't stay in that room for three more days." I was shaking and tearing up.

"We agree. We've been calling a few different places. We have an idea of where she could go, and we think it would be very beneficial to her. It's a wilderness therapy program called Aspen. It is twelve weeks in the wilderness. This program is similar to ours; they work on DBT and other forms of therapy. It's just in a different setting that I believe Lauren would benefit from. They have an opening; she could start tomorrow."

"That sounds great, but tomorrow . . . this is getting ridiculous. We've been waiting in Salt Lake for three days."

"I know. This process just takes a few days."

I rolled my eyes. "Can I even talk to her?"

"No, that is probably not a good idea."

"I will call the transporters and have them at Daybreak at eight in the morning," Jared said.

"That sounds good. We will have her ready. Meanwhile, Aspen is in Salt Lake, and you can talk to them and get the information you need."

"Tell her I love her, will you? Please?"

Jared called the transport company and I listened in. "Yes, she's fifteen," he said. "She weighs one hundred and eighty pounds and is five foot seven. No, she doesn't hit or punch. She yells, mostly.

Yes, she does have a history of running away. No allergies. Yes, she is on medications. They have a list of them. How does this all work, exactly?" Jared put the phone on speaker.

"Well," a nice-sounding man said, "we're a private company that is specially trained to handle disruptive people and also transport them. The doors have child locks, and they have the whole back-seat to themselves. Most kids listen to music or talk to us. There are always two transporters, and there will be a female there for Lauren."

"So you just drive them?"

"Yes, we will stop and get something to eat, and we do stop for bathroom breaks if we can trust the child to not run."

It was like I had a felon for a kid. "We pay you when we see you?" I felt like I was dealing with a smuggler of some kind.

"Yep, that will work," he said.

"Awesome. That is awesome," I said sarcastically, and hung up the phone. "I can't believe we have a complete stranger driving our daughter in a prison car for four hours."

I plugged Aspen into my GPS. It was just fifteen miles south on the main highway from where we were. "Surely the kids are not outside 24-7, right?" I asked Jared.

He shrugged his shoulders. "I wonder how much it costs."

We pulled into the parking lot. "It's a warehouse? What the heck?" We walked up to what appeared to be a small office.

"Hi," a woman said from behind the desk. "Can I help you?"

"Um, hi. I'm Kari, and this is Jared. Daybreak Academy was going to call about a Lauren Gusso."

"Oh, yes. We did just hear from them. Sounds like she is coming from Hurricane with a transporter."

I looked at Jared and whispered, "She says it as if it's everyday lingo around here."

"Can I get you a coffee or water?" she asked.

Jared nodded. "Coffee, please."

We walked into a nice little office and sat down. She came in and handed Jared the coffee. "Sammy will be here in a bit. He is our admission coordinator. He will answer questions and help with the paperwork."

"So how does this work, exactly?" I asked.

"Great question!" She seemed too excited about this. "Well, it's coed, but they are in groups with only boys or girls. The groups are between four and eight kids. During the week, one group might go biking, and another might go hiking or rock climbing. They have gear and everything they need to survive in the wilderness for seven days at a time. Each week they come back to base camp and shower, get a clean set of clothes and fresh supplies, and then are off again to a new destination."

My mouth must have been on the floor. "So they shower once a week?" I asked.

"Yep. They get five minutes. They have their cooking supplies and rations for themselves. They learn to cook and to take care of their garbage. They don't have a tent or pillows. They do have a large tarp and rope, a big, comfortable sleeping bag, and really good gear. They get new shoes about every two weeks, and we do foot checks three times a day. That's so they can get on top of a blister right away. The kids have raincoats, warm jackets, shorts or pants, socks, and underwear. They can get a ponytail holder if needed. They will do all their counseling and therapy right there, on the campsite. They carry all their supplies in a pack that they wear on their back. It weighs about sixty pounds. It is quite the workout. There is one staff member for every three kids. They do have a good time, and they learn a lot."

Sammy came in. "Hi," he said, and shook Jared's hand and mine in turn. "I have the paperwork for you. When Lauren gets here, she will go to the warehouse and get her gear; you can say a quick hi and goodbye, and then she'll leave with the team to go meet up with her group. Her group has four other girls and two staff. They are at the main camp this week. It's a training week, so Lauren will start at a perfect time."

He handed us the paperwork. The program was twelve thousand dollars a month. I could see the blood drain out of Jared's face. "Can we fill these out and bring them back tomorrow?" he asked. "I need to call our banker and get some things lined up."

"Yes, of course. I'll see you tomorrow at noon."

I followed Jared to the car. "This looks like a good program. Are you okay?" I asked.

"Just overwhelmed," he said. "Nothing new." It was his turn to crash.

After a good dinner and a good night's sleep, Jared had a better grip on how this was going to work financially. I was thrilled we were going to get to see Lauren today, even if it was for only a few minutes. I missed her dimples, her sense of humor, and her enormous heart.

When we arrived at the warehouse, they asked us to park on the road. They didn't want Lauren to see that there were other people here, possibly her parents. We would get to see her as long as she was cooperative. It was like she was in prison and might be released for good behavior.

The transporter car pulled up. Lauren stepped out and then disappeared into the warehouse. About thirty minutes later, Sammy came and said we could see her. We followed him into the back. It was enormous; there was a different section for water bottles, pants, shorts, tops, jackets, backpacks, shoes, socks, underwear, camping gear—anything you could think of and in any size needed.

Lauren was getting her pants and top on in the bathroom. I was hiding behind a shelf with boxes and boxes of boots. When Lauren came out, they let us go to her. I walked and stood about twenty feet in front of her. I didn't say anything. For about a second, it looked like she was trying to compute why I was there. Then she ran over to me and gave me a big hug. "Mommy," she said, starting to cry.

I held her and cried too. I didn't have the time to say all the things I wanted to say. I missed her smelly feet and her unshaven legs that I harped on her to shave. I missed her big brown eyes and her voice. I missed hearing her call me Mommy. I missed her busyness and the ideas she came up with that I would always try to curb. I missed her hunting for frogs and selling them to the neighbor kids. I just missed her.

"We gotta go," Sammy said.

"Wait," I said. I pulled out a candy bar, a Coke, and the book *Marley & Me*. "Here, this will give you something to do; it will probably be your last treat for a while." I looked into her big brown eyes. "Go learn, explore, and find yourself, Lauren. I know she is in there somewhere. Go get her."

She nodded her head. "I love you, Mommy."

"I love you too, Lauren. More than you'll ever know."

Lauren walked away with the wilderness staff.

For the next few days, I felt like a puppet on a string. I don't even remember getting back home to South Dakota.

Weeks drifted along. We were able to email Lauren every day, and they put pictures on their website every week. "Jared, there's a great picture of Lauren all wrapped up in her sleeping bag," I said as I giggled. "Oh my gosh, Jared, look at this. They're knee-deep in mud and muck! She's riding bikes and rock climbing . . ." I paused. She was smiling in every picture. I sat at my computer with a silly grin on my face.

Six weeks from the day we dropped her off, Jared and I headed to Utah for the parent seminar. "Did you ever think life would be like this?" I asked Jared in the rental car.

"What do you mean?" Jared asked, but I could tell he knew exactly what I meant.

"I'm just bummed, I guess. I've struggled with keeping a nursing job because of the time and energy it takes to care for Lauren. Having to run to the school or home on a moment's notice. Being on the phone dealing with a crisis and having my coworkers upset because I'm not available to help them. Crying at work because the stress of Lauren's behaviors is too much. Not being able to keep up with family, work, and Lauren. Having to take her to the hospital, never leaving her alone, locking doors, hiding meds, and hiding the Wi-Fi cord so there is no internet in the house. I've worked at the hospital, then the clinic, then the VA, then the hospital again. It's not what I planned when I went to nursing school, and nursing school sucked. A BSN was an extremely tough degree for me to get, only to stay home," I complained. "But I have no choice. Nobody asked me if I was okay with the cards I was dealt. It's just not what I planned, I guess." Jared just looked at me. I guess it was my turn to crumble, again. I guess I was in the angry stage at this point. I was mourning the loss of the life I wanted for my daughter.

At the seminar, I felt the same sense of community that I had at Daybreak. All the people there had been through some kind of struggle and torment with their own child. I felt strangely comforted knowing we had that in common. It felt like an exclusive club.

After four hours of class, sitting and listening to the lecture, I could hardly keep my eyes open. Then I heard a group of people coming in the back. I sat up straight. *Where is she?* I thought. All the teens looked identical: army-green hats, black T-shirts, army-green lightweight cargo pants with zippers at the knee, and black boots. They all were filthy. Tousled, messed-up hair in ponytails, noses and cheekbones pink from the sun, dirt spots on their knees—and "perma-dirt," as Lauren called it. That was the dirt that got under their skin. The dirt didn't wash off easily. They looked dirty all the time, even after their weekly shower. But they all seemed relatively happy.

"Mom!" Lauren yelled from across the room. I wrapped my arms around her dirty black shirt and gave her a big hug. "Lauren, you look so good!" She was filthy and smelled like a barn, but I didn't want to make her to feel bad. She was smiling, and that was all that mattered. The teacher announced that lunch was ready in the other room.

I didn't think I'd ever seen kids so happy to get a ham sandwich, chips, and fruit. "Oh my gosh. Milk!" Lauren said in delight. She devoured the carton of milk. "We drink water; sometimes we get Kool-Aid to mix in, but mostly water. We have to drink four liters a day."

"What do you eat?" I asked as I put a chip into my mouth.

"Rice and beans. I hate rice and beans, but that's all we eat. Oatmeal for breakfast, usually, and nuts, dried fruit, or chocolate chips for snacks. We pick those out right away when we get our rations for the week. The other day we had watermelon." All the girls sitting at the table with us sighed. "It was the best watermelon ever. We tore it open and used our hands to break it apart. Dinner is usually canned meat, rice, and beans, sometimes pasta. We carry everything around, so we don't have much. Dried food is the best for moving and packing."

Is this the kid that I couldn't get to wake up and go to school or do any chores at home?

The girls were talking a mile a minute, sharing jokes, and laughing. "How about the cow in the kitchen?" Lauren said as she giggled. All the girls at our table started laughing.

"What? A cow?" I said.

"Yeah, there was a bull about twenty yards from where we kept our food tied up in a tree. We all stood very still and the bull started to walk toward us slowly. We were paralyzed with fear. We looked at the staff, not quite sure what to do. The bull got closer, until it was standing in our makeshift kitchen. Then, very slowly, the staff yelled, 'Everyone run!' I guess the bull was doing that thing with his foot that they do before they charge. I think the yelling scared him away, 'cause he left." All the girls were laughing. "We even have a picture of it, Mom!"

"The poop bucket," another girl said, and all the kids started laughing and groaning at the same time.

"Come again? I must not have heard you right. Poop bucket?" As I said it, it dawned on me what they were talking about . . . *No way!*

"Yeah, Mom. When you have to poop, you have to pick it up with a baggy, and then it goes into the poop bucket. We can't just leave our poop lying on the ground."

I looked at her in utter disgust. "I never thought of that," I said, grossed out. "Who carries this bucket?" I asked.

"Whoever is making poor choices. It's usually me," Lauren said.

Of course it's you, I thought. "You'd better start making better choices, then."

"Lauren doesn't like to hike far places," a girl at the table said.

"Yeah we all had to wait forever when Lauren fake-died."

I literally laughed out loud. "What?"

"Lauren fake-dies when she doesn't want to go on and continue hiking. Then we all have to wait for her," she said in the monotone, like it was an everyday normal event. "She lies down and won't move or go any farther. One day she didn't drink any water, and she was faint, and they had to take her to the ER. That's why we say she fake-dies."

I was busting a gut. "I'm sorry," I said. "It's just the way you explained it, that is so funny." I could totally see Lauren lying on the ground, refusing to go any farther.

Next, we met Lauren's therapist, Alyssa. "Lauren struggles with direction, not knowing what to do," she said. "She also has trouble reading others' emotions and body language. She has had a few instances where she completely misunderstood something that was very minor, and it turned into WWIII."

"That makes sense. I've seen that behavior," I said. We continued to talk until our sixty minutes were up.

"This is your five-minute warning," a staff member said. "Then the kiddos and I are going back to roughing it."

"I don't want you to leave, Mommy," Lauren said. She was probably too old to be calling me that, but I didn't correct her. It made my heart melt all the same.

"I know, but you'll be home before you know it." I gave her a big hug. "You still smell like a barn." I kissed her rosy cheek and wrinkled my nose.

"I only get one lukewarm, ten-minute shower a week. What do you expect?" She was smiling when she walked away with her clan. I laughed out loud. *Her little clan*, I thought.

CHAPTER 26

LAUREN WAS HOME FOR the summer, and we had a plan. I had put out an ad looking for a caregiver, and we'd hired Ally and Celine. They were both teachers looking for some extra duties. Jared and I decided that Lauren really couldn't be alone, ever. The gals were hired to hang out with Lauren and assist her in decision making. "Lauren just needs some guidance and direction," I explained to them.

Nikki came running in the house. "Mom, Lauren caught a duck." "What?"

"We were at the park where they have that pond, and Lauren saw a momma duck and baby ducklings floating by, and she ran and leaped into the water and swam after the ducks until she caught one. She kept it for a little bit and then Ally made her put it back. Lauren was mad though. She went into the pond to get a turtle instead, and she came out covered in mud up to her armpits."

I didn't know whether to laugh or cry. "Well, tell her she needs to be hosed off. Ponds have a lot of bacteria." Just as Nikki said,

Lauren was covered in muddy muck; it was like she was coated in chocolate pudding. "Lauren, how could you have thought that this was a good idea?" I asked her.

"I wanted to catch a duck, and I did, but stupid Ally made me put it back."

"Stand in the front yard; I'm going to hose you off. Then you'll have to go in the garage and take off the pants and shirt. I don't want that tracked all over the house."

Lauren didn't seem to care much that the sitters were around her. She wanted to hang out with her own friends—but they left much to be desired. When you don't have a large pool to choose from, you take what you can get. Some were rough on the outside but had very kind hearts.

"Mom, can we drop off Ely?"

"Sure," I said. Ely had become a favorite of mine. She was super sweet and was a good friend to Lauren. Ely lived in a foster home. I wasn't sure of her situation, but it sounded like her mom was overwhelmed and had some other issues, so Ely had gone into foster care. Her brother had been shot and killed earlier in the year. My heart went out to this child. I turned the corner to her house.

"Oh, I changed houses," she said matter-of-factly.

"What? Where are you living now?"

"I was moved to another town; I had to change schools." She gave me the directions to her new house.

"How is your new school?"

"It's okay. I miss my old school," she said. "Turn left here. It's on the right. It's the one with the cars in the driveway."

I stared at the most run-down, sketchy house I'd ever seen. *I wouldn't let my dog go in there.* "Ely, are you going to be okay?"

"It's fine," she said as she got out of the car.

I looked at her, trying to have a silent conversation. She began to walk to the door. I wanted to put her back in the car and drive away. "Ely," I said, and she turned around. "Please call me if you need anything." She nodded.

We didn't see much of Ely again. Lauren heard she was back home with her mom in the party and drug scene. My heart broke for her.

Lauren had many friend situations like this, with little to no parental support or supervision of any kind. I was continually supervising these teens who were not accustomed to parents calling the shots. Kids were at our house, and I was seriously worried about being robbed. We started hiding things and locking office doors. Megan and Nikki were on edge also. Random people would show up at our home and Lauren would give me her "I don't know who they are" look.

We were hosting a bonfire one night with our neighbors, and a van of about ten boys pulled into the driveway. They all jumped out and started playing basketball and hanging out in the garage. Apparently, Lauren had a friend that was dating one of the boys.

She invited them in to watch a movie. I guess that was code for "You now have permission to come and run around my house." I had never encountered something like this; I didn't know what to do. I thought Jared was going to have an aneurysm. Finally, he and three other dads had to ask these kids to leave our property. I was scared. The kids piled back into the van and sped away. That van drove by our house for many days after that.

I tried to keep up with Lauren's social media. I didn't know how, but within ten minutes she could find random people, friends of friends, and have some social gathering concocted. She also had radar for picking out the worst kids. It all happened so fast that I never knew which end was up.

Lauren went to meet up with some kids, with our permission.

We were trying to test her to see if she was learning to make good choices, so this time she went without Ally or Celine. We drove her to meet up with her "friends" and told her she had to keep us updated on her whereabouts.

"Hi, Dad," Lauren said over the phone.

"Hi, Lauren."

"We're going to the grocery store, and then they will bring me home."

"Where are you guys now?"

"Um, we're on our way to the store."

"What store are you going to?"

"Umm . . ."

Little did Lauren know, we had an app that tracked her phone. "Lauren, I know you're at Fall's Park." Fall's Park could be sketchy at night. "Do you think you should be on your way home now?"

"Yes, Dad."

"Okay, see you soon." Fifteen minutes later, Jared called Lauren. "Hi, Lauren. Are you on your way home?"

"Yep, we are in the car driving."

"Lauren, I know you're still at Falls Park. Get on your way home now, or I am coming to get you."

"Okay, Dad. But how do you know where I am?"

"Oh, I have my ways."

Lauren made it home, safe and sound. I don't know if she ever caught on.

"Mom, can Celine pick up my friend Rory and take us to the mall?"

"I think that would be okay." Lauren said he was a friend she'd met at another gathering she had been at, that he was sixteen and in high school. That's why we hired these girls to provide twenty-four hour supervision for Lauren. I hadn't met Rory, but I never met any of Lauren's friends until they were at our door.

I gave Celine a twenty. "Get some ice cream or something. Lauren, stay with Celine and be good, okay?" She nodded, and they got in the car and left.

"Nikki, we need to leave for volleyball soon. Get your water bottle and knee pads and get in the car." My phone rang. It was Celine. I had the familiar feeling of dread I got every time my phone rang. I held the phone with my chin as I tried to get the car door open. "Hello?"

"Hi, Kari. Um . . ."

"Is everything okay?" I asked.

"No, not really."

"What happened?" Thoughts flew through my mind—*Oh no, she shoplifted. She ran away. She got into a fight.*

"Lauren went to the bathroom and was gone for about ten minutes. I walked back to the bathroom area, and she said she was okay. When she came out, she was wet from the waist down. I asked her what happened and she said that she and Rory had sex in the bathroom. She didn't want too, but he insisted."

What do you say when you're told your daughter was assaulted in a public restroom at a very busy mall with supervision?

Celine was beside herself. "I'm so sorry. I should have gone to the bathroom with her. She has gone before by herself and was fine. I had no idea Rory was going in the bathroom with her, and I was right in the food court."

"Celine, you didn't do anything wrong."

"Mom," Nikki asked, "is Lauren okay?"

"She's fine, hon."

"What do we do now?" Celine asked.

"Go to the ER, and I will meet you there." I dropped Nikki off with my sister-in-law and drove to the emergency room at the hospital where I worked. I saw people I knew as I walked to the special waiting room for assault victims. I walked into Lauren's room and said, "Really?"

Looking back, I probably could have been more compassionate. But I didn't know what to feel. I was mortified and pissed and sad and concerned. Lauren started crying.

"What the heck happened?" Obvious, but I needed to start somewhere.

"I didn't want to, Mom. He made me. He pushed me on the ground, and it hurt a lot. There was blood everywhere."

A nurse and a police officer had joined us. "What did you do with the blood?" the police officer asked.

"Nothing," Lauren said.

"You left the bathroom, and there was blood on the floor?" I asked, dumbfounded.

"Yes." She didn't seem to see the problem. The police immediately left for the mall.

Celine was in a chair crying. "What could have I done differently?" she asked.

"Listen," I said. "I wouldn't doubt that this was entirely planned by this asshole. He is a perpetrator. I would never have guessed something like this would even be possible." I walked Celine to the door and told her to go home, that I would keep her posted.

Tests were done, exams performed, and blood drawn. They took her pants and underwear. *Those are Pink-brand leggings*, I thought. *Those are expensive.* I wasn't sure if it was wrong for me to be thinking that. "Do we get those back?" I asked. I got a "No, you idiot, you don't get your pants back" look. *Okay, got it. Just checking*, I thought.

Lauren was able to "testify" through a program called Child's

Voice, which helps kids process a trauma. But the severity of what had happened to Lauren didn't hit her. I didn't know if she would ever truly comprehend what that horrible person stole from her that day, something that was hers and only hers to give away.

Lauren went on with her everyday antics. We sat in the front yard, enjoying the evening. Off in the distance, there were a few deer in a field. Lauren took off like a black lab hunting for a downed bird.

"What the hell? Lauren, come back here! You are not going to catch a deer." The deer were spooked and ran, and so did Lauren. *Crap*. I grabbed my keys and got in my van. Jared was out of town, and the other kids were at home and had no idea I just left. I drove up and down the streets of our neighborhood, following Lauren as she ran after the deer. I turned up my Christian music, sat back, and looked out the window.

CHAPTER 27

PRESENT DAY

"How much longer?" Lauren asked from the backseat. The sun was bright and shining into the car, making it warm and cozy, but she and Milo were getting antsy in the back.

"We're almost to Salt Lake," I told Lauren. My phone rang, and I answered it while Jared drove. "Hello?"

"Hi, Kari, this is Sammy at Aspen. I understand that you are bringing Lauren out here to come back to wilderness therapy."

"That was our plan," I said. "Is there a problem?"

"Well," Sammy said, "the gal you talked to didn't have all the information. We feel that Lauren has done our program and we feel that she wouldn't get much out of repeating it. Also, with all of Lauren's aches and pains, and not knowing if it is psychosomatic, we're hesitant to bring her back. Have you found anything out about her abdominal pain?"

"I have taken her to the doctor, and we didn't get an answer, just pain with unknown etiology."

"Because we don't know what's going on, we think that Aspen is not the best fit right now for Lauren."

"We just drove nineteen hours, and we're about thirty miles out of Salt Lake. What am I supposed to do now? Her school will not take her back until she has some treatment. We just want her to be able to go back to Brooks Academy."

"Let me do some looking," Sammy said. "Maybe there is another program in Salt Lake that would fit the requirement for her to return to her school."

I took a deep breath. "If you could do that, that would be helpful."

Jared looked at me and knew what I was going to say. "Are you serious?"

"Apparently, the gal that accepted Lauren back to Aspen Wilderness Therapy didn't know the whole story. They are concerned about her abdominal pain. That was a major issue the last go-around, having to leave the wilderness program and take her to the ER. They don't want to have to do that again."

"I don't get to go to Wilderness?" Lauren popped up from the back seat. "I want to go to Wilderness."

"I don't think it's going to work, Lauren. They are concerned about your abdominal pain. They are looking for another program."

"I don't want another program; I won't go. You can't make me go."

I turned to Jared. "Why does this always have to be so fucking complicated, all the time?"

Aspen eventually called back. "Hi, Kari, this is Sammy from Aspen. We found another option for Lauren. There is a really good facility called Point of View. We called them and gave them Lauren's information. They are expecting your call."

"Okay, thanks." I was deflated. I knew this was going to be a nightmare.

Lauren had been quiet in the back. "Mom?" she said.

"Yeah, Lauren?" I answered.

"I thought about what heaven would be like. Do you believe that Jesus is waiting for us when we get there? I bet he and God will be waiting with big posters that say my name. Like the guys in the airport when you get off the plane. It will be so cool. They will be so happy to see me and cheer. All the people will cheer because, in heaven, everyone belongs. No one is left out or feels different. I will have friends that don't want to hurt me. I won't have to always say goodbye to you. I hate when you leave me places. I don't want to be left again. I'm a person too, with feelings."

What are we going to do? I thought.

Jared pulled into the parking lot of Point of View. I faked a smile and got out of the car.

It was a beautiful day, cloudy but still slightly warm. There were no kids playing outside. *That's a shame*, I thought. *Kids should be running around outside today.* There was an eerie sense of quiet. The sidewalk leading to the main door was very long. Double glass doors led us to a reception area. There was a desk right away, and to the left was a door, which I guessed was locked. The doors were always locked.

"Mom, I don't want to stay here," Lauren said as she held on to my shirt.

"I know, Lauren, but I don't know what else to do. You just need to get through this so that you can go back to Brooks Academy."

A lady came out to meet us. "Hi, this must be Lauren," she said.

"Yes, we were referred to Point of View by Aspen." The locked door magically opened, and we were escorted into the unit. There was a hallway for boys and a hallway opposite for the girls. There were residents walking around, and others were watching TV.

"Lauren, do you want a tour?" The lady asked. Lauren looked at me.

"Sure, we would love to see the unit," I answered for Lauren.

Everyone had their own room and bathroom. "The rooms seem nice, Lauren. They're private and you have a nice window." I tried to point out the positives. "The bed seems soft." I sat down on what would be her bed. Lauren sat down next to me.

"Kari, we should probably get going," Jared said gently. He knew what was coming, and it was inevitable. *Just pull the bandage off fast, right?*

Lauren grabbed my shirt and held on for dear life. She looked at me with these big brown eyes in a total panic. "Mommy, please, please don't leave me here. Take me with you."

A staff member escorted Jared out, and two more men came up to Lauren and me. They seemed nice, trying to talk Lauren down. "Lauren, your mom needs to leave now." *No, I don't,* I wanted to say. *I'm taking her with me.* Lauren released my shirt. *What, how did that happen?* I saw that one of the workers had used a pressure point to get her to release the grip. I fell to the ground, sobbing.

Lauren was on the floor being held down by these men. She was screaming, "Mommy, no!"

What is happening? Is this right? Am I supposed to fight for her back? I was taken out into the hallway on the other side of the locked door. I vomited in the garbage. "I can't do this," I told Jared.

"We just need to leave. She'll be okay when we leave."

I could hear Lauren cry as we walked out the double glass doors.

I got in the van. I was sobbing and furious with Jared for not taking my side. I needed to throw up again. I grabbed a bag that was on the floor and dry heaved. Jared put the car in drive and we started the nineteen-hour drive home. Milo was in the backseat looking out the window, probably wondering where his human was.

CHAPTER 28

ALL I REMEMBER DOING for the two weeks after we got home was crying. I couldn't get anything done. We didn't get to talk to Lauren much, but we did get letters. Her letters were concerning; she said they were mean and unfair and didn't listen to the kids.

The plan was that Point of View would do a complete assessment and testing to help us understand Lauren a little better so we could help her emotionally. I was trying so hard to trust the process and let them do their job, but I needed to see her. I wanted her to know that we were rooting for her, that she wasn't alone in this. And I had a mama-bear feeling that something was wrong. Jared reluctantly agreed, and I flew out to see Lauren.

I talked to Lauren's therapist, and they granted her off-campus privileges while I was there. She just had to be back to Point of View by six o'clock. I went to the facility, walked through the glass doors, and was able to go through the locked door. Lauren gave me a big hug. She looked okay; maybe my maternal instincts were off.

We spent the day walking and shopping in downtown Salt Lake and had a late lunch of pizza. By the time we got back, Lauren had missed dinner, and I asked the staff if she could put her leftover pizza in the fridge and eat it later if she was hungry. The staff were totally fine with that, and they put her name on the box. I kissed Lauren goodbye.

This might just be okay, I thought. I showered, finished my leftover pizza, watched TV, and went to sleep. I slept well.

I was told I could come back at ten in the morning, so I took my time getting ready and sipping my coffee. I had a hop in my step; the sun was out and it was a beautiful day. I walked through the glass doors and noticed the lady we saw when we first brought Lauren to Point of View. She unlocked the door, and I walked into the unit. Everyone was looking at me.

Lauren walked up to me and started to cry. "What happened? What did I miss?" I said.

"I wanted to eat my pizza, and they told me that it was gone and staff ate it. I was mad. That is not okay, Mom. I told them they were not supposed to eat my pizza. So they restrained me, and they hurt my wrist."

There must be a misunderstanding. I took a deep breath and asked the staff, "Is there someone I can talk to?"

They just stared at me.

"Is there someone in charge?"

A young woman walked up to me. "I'm the nurse," she said.

"Can we go somewhere private, please?" I asked. We walked into her office. "What the heck is going on?" I asked.

"I don't know. I wasn't here last night."

"Can you ask about the pizza deal? Is this true? What happened with the restraint?"

"I told you: I was not here last night. I don't know."

"You're the nurse, and you don't know what happened last night when one of your residents was restrained and has a sore wrist? Did she hit her head? Is the restraint documented?"

She just stared at me. I walked out of the office. As I walked out into the main area, I saw three very intimidating male staff members. I walked back into the nurse's office and said, "I'm pulling her. Give me what I need to sign."

I was gathering what few things Lauren had, and I heard a commotion. I looked up. Lauren was down the boys' hall, saying goodbye to another resident, and one of the men was yelling at her to move. "I just want to say goodbye to Sam," Lauren said.

I thought the man was going to restrain her right here and now in front of me. "Lauren, get over here now." I signed what I needed to sign, and we left. I looked at Lauren and said, "I will never leave you again. I promise."

Lauren was holding her wrist; it did appear somewhat swollen. "Does it hurt?" I asked.

"Yeah. They held me down and pushed my wrist up against my back. I kept telling them they were hurting me. I told you they were not nice."

"Do you think we should have your wrist looked at?"

Lauren nodded.

We had an X-ray done, and a doctor came into the room and told us her wrist was indeed injured. She said she wasn't sure if it was a ligament or a small fracture. We needed to follow up with an orthopedic doctor. My head was spinning. I had left my daughter at a place that had hurt her, and I had left her there on purpose. She had cried, "Mommy, please don't leave me here." But I had. And there was nothing she could do but wait for me to come back.

Baby girl, I thought, *someday you will see your loving kingdom. Someday you will feel welcomed and loved by everyone. Someday you'll be forever safe.*

Lauren and I flew home. It was bad timing; Megan's cheerleading team was headed to Summit, the largest competitive cheer competition of the year—at Disney World. There would be a lot of commotion, people, and downtime, and Lauren needed twenty-four hour supervision. She would not do well there.

"Hey, Lauren," I called to her. "Would you like to go to Grandma Jane's for a few weeks while Megan and I are at Summit?"

Her eyes grew big. "Yeah, I would love that. Can Milo come?"

"No, he has to stay home with Dad."

"I want Milo to come too. I need a dog at Grandma's."

"Jake will be there." Jake was my parents' black lab.

"No. I want Milo." We had this conversation about twenty times before we left.

Florida was hot. It was May, and there were thousands of cheerleaders and spectators. We stood in line for hours to get our passes and lanyards. I was sweating so much, and my forehead hurt. I could see a few bumps appearing. "I never get acne on my forehead; this is so strange," I told Megan. She looked at me like she was wondering why I thought she would care. The girls had practices and team dinners. Cheer competitions were a place where you hurried up to just wait. On the first day of the competition, I woke up with even more pain on my forehead. I looked in the mirror, and the handful of bumps were not red anymore; they were black.

Enfuego, Megan's team, rocked the floor with a zero-deduction routine. For the first time in the history of South Dakota gyms, Dakota Spirit Enfuego made it into the top ten and advanced to day two. Everyone was elated. As we were waiting for the girls to change, I asked a fellow parent, who happened to be a physician, about my head. He said it looked like shingles.

I stared blankly at him. "How did I get that?"

"Stress," he said.

"You don't say." Figures.

Megan's team came in ninth. The bumps on my head scabbed and eventually went away, but they left a scar. *Great*, I thought. *Now I have a reminder of the horrific past two months.*

Lauren was still at my parents' and was doing well, but they were getting tired. Lauren was seen by an orthopedic doctor in Florida, who after seeing her X-rays said it was indeed fractured. So Lauren got a very pretty blue hard cast for the summer. Lauren was obsessed with getting a dog. "Play with Jake," I told her. Lauren was bummed having a hard cast on her arm from her hand to her elbow. This eliminated many of the things that would otherwise keep her occupied. The summer was just starting, and we had no idea what the plan was for Lauren.

I was walking to my car when my phone rang. It was Lauren's phone. "Hi, Lauren," I said.

"Mom, I'm mad." Lauren was strangely calm. "I took Grandpa's golf cart, and I'm going to the dog park," she said.

"Where are Grandma and Grandpa?" I asked. I couldn't figure out what the problem was.

"They're at home," she stated.

"Do they know that you have the golf cart?" Just then, my mom beeped in. "Hello," I said.

"Hi, has Lauren called you?"

"Yeah, I'm on the phone with her now. She said she has the golf cart and is going to the dog park. What's going on?"

"I'm going to drive to the dog park," Mom said.

"Okay." I beeped over to the other line. "Lauren, is everything okay?"

She was quiet. "Mom, I want a dog." Lauren had this way of

becoming obsessed with a subject, and it could take her a while to move on.

"Lauren, we can't get a dog. Grandma is coming to the dog park to see if you are okay."

"Mom." Lauren paused. "I'm not at the dog park."

"Where are you, then?" I wasn't even surprised.

"I'm at the grocery store. I bought a dog on Craigslist, and they are meeting me at the grocery store by Grandma's house."

I lost connection. *Damnit.* I switched lines and told my mom what was happening.

"What?" my mom yelled.

"Lauren is at the grocery store picking up a dog she bought on Craigslist."

"I'm on my way. I can't believe I let this happen." She was starting to cry.

"It's not your fault. Just get Lauren and we'll figure this out. Have Lauren call me when you get home."

"What should I do about the dog?" she asked.

"No idea," I told her with a sigh.

I tried to be productive at home, but I was just walking in circles around my house. *It's been too long*, I thought. I decided I would just call them. "What is going on?" I asked my mom.

"Well, things are not going great here," she said. She sounded upset, but more stressed than sad. "Lauren was at the grocery store with a couple that looked like they were straight out of a reality show. They had lots of tattoos, and the woman had a big yellow snake around her neck. Their car was beaten up, and they were just sketchy." Anyone with a tattoo is sketchy to my mom. "When I got there, Lauren had already purchased the dog, and I was not about to ask them about their return policy. We left and parked in another part of the parking lot to talk about the dog. She was fine, just mostly upset that I wouldn't let her keep the puppy. I told her we needed to take it to the shelter. She said that she bought the dog because she saw the dog on Craigslist and it looked abused. She knew I wouldn't let her get it, so she went and did it on her own."

"As we were visiting the shelter, a little girl and her mom came up to us and started playing with the puppy. We started talking to them and told them the story, and they decided that they would take the puppy home."

"So everything was fine?" I asked.

"Not really," Mom said hesitantly. "When we got home, Lauren went to the bathroom to take a shower. I didn't think anything of it. She was in there for a while, so I went to check on her, and she was covered in blood." Mom started crying. "She had a razor in the bathroom and cut up her arm. I'm trying to get the bleeding to stop. She may need stitches."

I tried to stay calm for Mom, even though I was panicking inside. "Mom, you need to take her to the ER."

"She may not need stitches."

"Mom, Lauren needs to be in the hospital. She needs to be assessed by a mental health professional."

"I know," she said.

"No, I don't want to go to the hospital," I heard Lauren say.

"How did this happen?" my mom said. "I wasn't mad at Lauren. We talked about the whole thing. We gave the dog to the little girl. I thought everything was fine."

"Mom, Lauren has so much more going on. This really isn't about the dog. She feels out of control. I'll fly out tomorrow. Take her to the ER and then call me."

Mom sounded defeated. "This is so hard; I don't know how you do this every day."

"I put one foot in front of the other," I answered.

But I was panicking. Lauren had been hospitalized ten times at the mental health hospital. She'd had multiple medication changes. We did therapy for her and for our family. Our school district had nothing they could offer her. She'd had eight school placements in the last two years. She was seventeen but only had four high-school credits. We sent her to Daybreak for sixteen months, but the wheels still fell off when she came home. I had been forced to leave multiple jobs because I couldn't keep up with work and family. Megan and Nikki were emotionally distraught, what with all the yelling and behavior at home. We lost friends and family connections because of the mental instability. We needed to do something different and rather drastic.

I sat Jared down and explained the situation to him. "Do you remember, at Daybreak, a lot of those parents talked about an educational consultant?"

Jared looked at me like I had discovered gold. I had been given a referral. We were both grasping for anything that would maybe help.

"Should I call and get some information?"

"It might be a good idea," Jared said.

I spent some time researching and did eventually call an educational consultant. Jeff came highly recommended and worked for a great firm. He was a tremendous help. I gave him Lauren's history and sent him her records so he could start to research schools. Educational consultants are very similar to realtors; they know all the schools and programs and come up with a list of needs from kids' records. He would then give us school options that best fit her needs. Unfortunately, Jeff was not cheap.

"Mom, why do you have to go? We planned on shopping together. It's not fair," Megan said. Nikki was reading a book on the couch. "This sucks. We can never do anything. Lauren always ruins everything."

I gave Megan a look. She stormed down to her room.

"What is she so upset about?" Jared asked as he came in through the garage door.

"We were going to go to Minneapolis and shop at the mall, but now I need to go to my parents' and figure out the plan for Lauren."

"Ahhhh," Jared said. "I'll talk to her. She'll be fine."

Nikki remained quiet on the couch, but I could tell she wasn't reading her book. She wouldn't speak up even if I asked her to.

"I spoke to the ed consultant. He's in the process of talking to schools. He mentioned that he thought Lauren may need a stay at an acute facility before she can go to any school. He's afraid she is not stable enough right now."

Jared was fiddling with his watch. "This stupid thing won't stay latched," he complained.

I looked at Nikki. "Hey, Nik, do you have any questions about me flying to see Lauren for a few days?"

"Nope."

My mom was waiting at the airport when I landed. On my way to meet her, I sidetracked into a Starbucks. *Coffee first.* I opened the back door of her car and threw my bag in the backseat.

"Hi." I leaned over to give Mom a hug.

"I'm so sorry. This is all my fault. I should have just let her get a dog," she whispered.

"Mom, look at the bigger picture. Lauren needs help. What did the hospital say?"

Mom explained all the things that I already knew. Mental health—yep; school—got it. Nutrition—okay; therapy—covered. It's always the same information, being told to me like I had no idea she was mentally ill. I supposed they would throw in a sticker chart to help. *Great. Thumbs up!*

We drove to the hospital to see Lauren. There were a few other kids who were also inpatients. It didn't seem crowded, and it was clean and bright. A little sterile, but it *was* a hospital.

Lauren peeked her head out of her room. "Hi, Mommy."

I touched her bandaged arm and looked into her big brown eyes. "A dog?"

"Sorry."

The nurse walked in. "Lauren, how are you feeling?"

"Good," she answered.

"Great. The doctor is discharging you."

Before long, we were walking out the door. I explained the consultant to Mom and Lauren. "He's thinking a short-term stay at facility might be better than going straight to a school."

"I don't want to go to treatment again. Mom, you promised that you would never leave me at a hospital again. You lied."

"I know, Lauren. This has been tough. Brehm told us that you going to school there is not an option. Dad and I don't know what else to do. I don't know where you are going to school this fall. There are so many other issues that Dad and I can't fix."

"I'm not going to school. I hate school. I don't need school."

I sighed.

The consultant called and gave us some options. The top pick was a well-known mental-health facility in Houston. Lauren and I flew out the next day. I was now a pro at booking tickets and rental cars. I had the process down pat.

The facility was big, clean, and homey. The air conditioning worked well, which was important because Houston was hotter than it ever got in the Midwest. Doctors, residents, and therapists all asked us the same questions.

We followed the admission counselor through the locked doors and into the adolescent unit. *Click.* There were about fifteen teens sitting around in a circle. I was having flashbacks to Lauren's stay at Point of View, to promising Lauren I would never leave her again.

Visiting hours were ending. "Mom, no, I don't want you to leave. I'm scared." Lauren was clinging to me. I didn't want them to restrain her, especially after the last placement where they broke her wrist. The staff noticed and were closing in on us. They seemed to be on the same page, not wanting to lay hands on her. "I don't want you to go. I love you. I'll be good, I promise." The nurse came over and gave Lauren a pill.

How can I get her out of here? I thought. I tried concocting a plan. *She doesn't have to live at home. We'll just get a one-bedroom apartment; it will be fine.*

"Lauren," said the nurse. "Mom needs to leave now."

I felt a hand on my back, leading me out the door. *Wait, what's going on? I can't leave her. Get her!* I thought. *Lauren, run! I'll help you.* But the words wouldn't come out of my mouth. My legs walked me out the door. *Why can't I stay and console my daughter? When Megan was in the hospital, I didn't leave her side. I hate mental health.*

Lauren cried, "Jesus wouldn't leave me!" The door closed. *Click.* I fell to my knees and cried. *I am always crying.*

CHAPTER 29

ALL IN ALL, THE facility in Houston was a holding place. They changed some of Lauren's medication. They did some tests and watched her for three weeks. Jeff found us a school two hours north of Salt Lake. I called him to update him on Lauren's discharge. He updated us and was in contact with our school district, helping coordinate the funding.

"The school doesn't have a spot for her yet," he told me. "But I don't think it's a good idea to take her home."

"Are you kidding? I'm not leaving her here until the school is ready."

He didn't sound pleased, but at the end of the day I was the mom, and I was paying him. Not that I had any idea what I was doing.

Home went as well as it could. "Lauren, you need to clean your room."

"I will! Mom, can I go with Tracy to the fair?"

Tracy was not trustworthy and definitely not a good influence. I couldn't trust these kids to make good choices. "You can go to the fair if Dad or I go with you." She looked at me with a scowl. "You know the rules, Lauren."

I could hear Lauren try to explain the rules to Tracy. She had lost cell phone privileges, so she used mine. "Mom," Lauren said, "you are making me have no friends."

"Is Tracy able to go?" I asked.

"Yes. I told her we would pick her up on Saturday at ten."

Nothing has changed, I thought. *We're still the chauffeur.*

Friday around three o'clock, Lauren asked if we could go to the fair to see just the animals. Jared volunteered to come too. *This will be fun,* I thought. *Lauren will get some Mom and Dad time.* As we were driving to the fair, I heard my phone buzz. It was a text from Tracy: *Hey Lauren can you go to the fair tonight instead. All my friends are going tonight. If I go tonight, my dad will say I can't go tomorrow with you.*

I gave Lauren my phone. "Can I please go with the kids tonight?" she asked.

"Only if Dad is with you."

Jared gave me the "Thanks for volunteering me" look.

"Mom." Lauren started to cry. "You are ruining my life."

"Lauren, the fair is probably the last place I would let you go off with these kids." It was probably for the best that Tracy cancelled on Lauren.

Lauren threw my phone at me.

Jared parked the car. I could see Lauren starting to spiral. I thought about going home right then and there, but I thought that maybe the animals would be good for her to see.

This fair was far trashier than most county fairs. I couldn't see any vendors. We went to the kiddy farm, and it was closed. We started walking to another barn and saw a litter of puppies with their mother.

Lauren went right up to them and snuggled a puppy. "Mom, I want this puppy."

Here we go, I thought. "No, Lauren, we are not getting a puppy."

"Why?" she said loudly. She was pissed.

"Seriously, Lauren, we're not getting another dog. We have two dogs at home."

She set the puppy down in its cage. She walked around, not looking at anything. "You know, if I could have gone with my friends, then I wouldn't be mad right now. It's all your fault."

I took a deep breath. I looked at Jared with a "Let's leave now" expression.

In these situations I've learned that, if I just walk away, Lauren will follow. Usually to yell at me.

"Where are all the animals?" she yelled at Jared and me.

"I don't know. Jared, was there no 4H this year?"

"Not sure," he responded. "We need to get out of the fair before she blows up," he said to me quietly. I walked faster.

"Where are you going?" Lauren said. "Goddamn it, stop, you're going too fast!"

I kept walking.

"You're a bitch!"

I could feel the other parents stare at me. I kept walking.

"I hate you; you made me mad."

I walked up to the car, unlocked it, and got in the backseat as fast as I could.

Lauren got in front with Jared. "You know this is your fault. You are such a bitch," she yelled.

"Lauren, do not talk to your mom like that."

"Shut up, asshole!" she yelled.

Jared started driving out of the park, onto the main roads, and out to the highway. I felt somewhat relieved that we were away from people and contained in a car. Lauren was coming unglued.

"Lauren, calm down."

"I hate my life. I'm gonna kill myself. I hate you. You are so mean." She started hitting herself on the head with her fist.

"Lauren, stop. You're going to hurt yourself."

She started taking the car apart. She dug her nails into the dash and scratched like a cat. We were almost home.

I got my phone out and texted Megan and Nikki: *Lauren is melting, go to your rooms and close the doors.* We pulled into the driveway. Jared got out and went in the house. I had no idea what to expect from Lauren at this time. Anything could happen. There was no way I was going to get her to take an "as needed" medication to relax.

Lauren grabbed the dash and opened the glove compartment. She tore the glove compartment off the car. I was stunned. Then she kicked the door, hyperextending it to the point that it was literally off the car.

I went inside. There was nothing I could do in these situations except keep her and others safe. She would eventually come down from her rage, but it could take three to four hours. She would walk into her room and slam the door. She would come out and pace around the house, like a lion in a cage, waiting for a chance to attack. She was bigger and stronger than me.

Jared and I walked around the house with her, trying to stay out of the way of slamming doors. We watched her every move. If she grabbed a bottle of pills or a sharp object, we would wrestle it out of her hand.

"How long is this going to last?" Jared asked me.

"I don't know; I'm not a fortune teller." I was mad that he was even asking.

"Lauren, can you calm down? Sit on the couch," Jared said.

She walked over to a bar stool and picked it up.

"Don't you dare!" Jared yelled. "Not in my house!" He looked like a ringleader, whip in hand, trying to make the lions nervous.

Lauren stared him down and stomped into her room. "I hate you!" she screamed at the top of her lungs. She slammed her door so violently that the whole door frame, door still attached, fell off the wall.

Jared looked at me and said, "If you don't call the police, I will."

All the hair on my body stood straight up.

CHAPTER 30

THE DOOR FALLING APART was enough to jolt Lauren out of her funk. She looked at the door. "Oh," she said.

"Lauren, get in the car now," I ordered. I grabbed her meds, she grabbed Milo, and we left in the van. I had enough adrenaline running through me that I felt I could do almost anything. My first reaction was to drive to Salt Lake tonight. I got on I-90 and headed west. I didn't have anything other than what I was wearing, my purse, and Lauren's meds.

"Mom, where are we going?" Lauren asked timidly. She was back to rational thinking and knew she had messed up.

"Lauren, we are driving to Salt Lake, where your new school is." Lauren was not willing to go to another school. Jared and I didn't know exactly how we were going to get her to school. I took this opportunity to make my move.

"How long does it take to get there?" she asked.

Good question. I was wondering that myself. Now I was even more frustrated.

My cell was buzzing. It was Auntie Kelly. "Can you answer that, Lauren?"

"Hi, Kelly." Lauren sounded less than enthused. She handed me the phone, and I put it on speaker.

"Hey, how are you?" my sister asked.

"Well, I think I'm driving to Salt Lake."

"What? Why?"

I explained the situation to Kelly.

"Kari, you can't drive to Salt Lake tonight. Pull over, and let's look at airline tickets." I could hear her tapping. "You can fly out of Omaha tomorrow morning at five thirty. It's a direct flight to Salt Lake."

"I have the damn dog," I mumbled to Kelly.

"Can you take Milo home?" she asked.

"I thought about it, but I don't think I want to give Lauren the option to go home. I would have to start the battle all over again. She needs the fewest amount of transitions possible if I'm going to get her to Salt Lake." A plan was forming in my mind. "I'm going to pull over and book those tickets. Then I'm going to drive to Omaha. It's three hours, and then we'll just go and hang out at the airport and maybe sleep. I'll have to call Jeff and have him set up a meeting with the school tomorrow. I'll call you later. Thank you for helping me."

The night wasn't horrible, but we didn't get any sleep. We were able to go through security at about four in the morning. We got the bulkhead seats, and I tried to sleep, but Milo had other thoughts.

"Mom can we go to Walmart and get a few things?" Lauren asked. In our rush out the door, we had brought almost nothing.

"Okay. We'll have to stop at some point," I told Lauren. I heard back from Jeff, and he set up a meet-and-greet tour at noon.

Lauren could start the next day.

We pulled up to the school and parked. There were three or four buildings that were all brick and well kept. There were wide sidewalks and lots of green grass. Boys ran across the grassy field playing a game. We toured the school, the office, the grounds, and the therapy rooms.

"The campus is three-quarters male," our guide told us. "The girls are housed at a private house, which the school staffs and runs." Lauren seemed impressed by the house. She wasn't running away, at least—I took that as impressive.

The first thing Lauren said to me the next morning was, "I don't want to stay here."

I closed my eyes and took a deep breath. "You need to give it a try. This is where our school district wants you to go to school; I don't have anywhere else for you to go. Sioux Falls has nothing they can offer us as far as assistance."

"Nope," she said digging in her heels. "I don't need to go to school."

Okay, glad you're flexible, I thought. "Lauren, please get in the car. I will drive you to school."

"Absolutely not. Nope. No. You will leave, and I will cry."

Biting my lip, holding back the tears, I tried to talk to her about school. She was not interested one bit. "How about the dog park?" Milo needed to run anyway.

She perked up. "Okay," she said quietly.

Lauren was calm at the park. Dogs, especially Milo, helped her with her emotions. It was nine o'clock, and there were a few people at the dog park. It was made half of grass and half of dirt paths that the dogs ran over and over. There was a chain-link fence surrounding the grassy area.

"Mom, you know when you are in front of a crowd, and you

have to give a speech, how nervous you feel?"

"Yeah, like throwing up," I said.

"That is how I feel every day. Every day I want to crawl out of my skin."

"Lauren, I'm so sorry," I said as I rubbed her back. "I can't imagine how that must feel. Do you think medication helps you?"

"It makes me really tired. It helps, but I'm so tired." Lauren took Milo off his leash. "There you go, Milo." Milo went running up to a few dogs that were sniffing each other.

For about a half hour, we shuffled toward the car, which was about five hundred feet from the entrance of the dog park. "Lauren, you can do this. We don't have a choice. This is who can help you." Lauren was crying and starting to amp up. I needed to get her to school now, or at least in the car. I opened the door, and Milo jumped in.

"I'm not getting in the car," she said loudly. People at the park started to look. I had the panicked feeling that I got when Lauren was going to lose it. Milo was shaking in the backseat. He got very nervous when Lauren was upset.

"Please, I need you to do this."

"Mom, I'm not staying here. I'm not going to school."

"Please sit on the seat; please get in the car."

"I just want to go home," she begged. I could see a couple staring at us.

"Come on, Lauren. Someone is going to think you are in trouble and call the police. Get in the car."

"No!" She yelled.

About thirty minutes passed, and finally a woman came over. "Is everything okay?" she asked.

"I want to go home," Lauren said, crying.

"Where is home, honey?" the woman asked.

"South Dakota," Lauren answered.

"Why are you here?" she asked.

"Yeah, Lauren," I said. "Why are you here?"

"Shut up, Mom."

I did my best to explain to the nice, very nosy, out-of-bounds woman. She seemed to understand, and she wished us well and went back to her car. I finally got Lauren into the car, put it in reverse, and locked the doors. We only had to go about three blocks to get to the school. Lauren tried to open the door.

"Lauren, stop!" I yelled.

She was in full meltdown mode. There was no reasoning with her now. As I drove into the parking lot of the school, I called the office and tried to talk. "Please, can someone help me? I'm in the parking lot with Lauren. She's really upset." Three staff members were outside immediately.

The school knew that Lauren had a history of restraint abuse, so the staff was trying very hard to not restrain her. Milo was already in the front seat, basically on my lap as I put the car in park. I opened my door, and Milo jumped out. Lauren was in the backseat, hitting the seat, hitting her head with her fist, screaming, kicking, and keeping the doors locked, I had the key. The staff tried to coerce her out of the car. I looked to them for direction. "What should I do?" I pleaded. I sat down on the pavement. "I can't do this," I whispered. "I can't do this!" I said louder, and stood up.

The staff looked at me. "What? Why? Where are you going to go?"

"I'm just going to take her home. I can't do this anymore. I'll call you and let you know where we are and what our plans are." I unlocked the car door and sat in the driver's seat. "Lauren, calm down. We are leaving." I turned right onto the highway and started driving to Salt Lake.

Lauren was quiet now, sitting in the back and looking at me, Milo next to her. "What are we doing, Mom?" Lauren asked.

"Going home," I answered. As I drove, I started daydreaming. I could cross the center line and get in a fatal accident, and all this would go away. I prayed, *Please, God, please help me, show me where to go, what I should do*. I sobbed and tried to stay on the road. *Stop. I needed to stop.* I looked around to find my bearings. I saw a McDonald's and pulled off the highway.

Lauren sat up in the backseat. "What are we doing? she asked. She had fallen asleep, felt the car stop, and woke up."

"I need a Coke," I said, exhausted. *What am I doing?*

"Can I get a Coke too?" she asked.

I nodded. "Did you take your noon medication?" I asked.

Suddenly, a strong wave of peace come over me. I was calm. I was told what I needed to do. Something stronger was moving me. I got Lauren's noon meds out and added an additional anti-anxiety pill. I felt that giving her another pill would still be safe, and I needed her to relax and sleep for the duration of the drive.

I went through the drive-through, ordered two Cokes, and pulled into a parking spot. I gave Lauren the drink and her pills. For a second, I wondered if she would notice the extra pill and call me out. Without a second look, she took her noon meds. We talked for a few minutes and listened to some music. She finished her Coke and put her head back on the jacket pillow she had made. I slowly started driving, heading northbound.

"Where are we going?" Lauren asked, half asleep.

"To the airport," I said. With no visible emotion, I lied to my child. My gut wrenched as I spoke.

"We went the wrong way on the highway," Lauren said.

"No, we're good." I hoped she wouldn't sit up and examine

where we were.

She went back to sleep.

My phone was on silent, but I saw a text come through from Jeff. *Where are you? Lauren needs to be at school, I promise you they can and will help her.* Still driving, I responded: *I'm on my way back.* If I was going to be somewhat successful at my plan, I needed her to stay asleep. I texted the staff too, telling them I was coming back to school and asking if they could meet me halfway. They agreed, and we worked out a plan. *What am I doing?* I went through the motions as my body moved, but I wasn't the one moving it; something else was.

I texted the staff that I was at the thirty-mile mark. I pulled off the highway into a very small rural town with dirt roads. I was scared to slow down, panicked Lauren would wake up. I found a circle drive and looped through it until I saw their car.

They pulled up, coming toward us, and I pulled up as close as I could parallel to their car. Lauren's door was blocked. I got out of my car. Two staff members jumped in the front, one in the back.

Lauren shot up. "What is happening? Mom where are you going?"

I stood on the gravel road, totally numb, as I watched my rental car with my baby in the backseat drive away. All I could see was Lauren looking at me through the back window as the car got smaller and smaller until it disappeared.

I sat down on the gravel road. "Please, God, help me, help her," I said out loud. "Thank you for getting me through that." I had to put 100 percent faith in the decision I made that moment. I cried and cried. The staff stayed with me until someone drove back with my car.

"She is fine. She talked with us the whole way back. She is at school getting settled. It's okay; you did well."

All I could say was, "I'm trusting you, please take care of her." I crawled back into my rental car, waved, and drove away without my Lauren. Milo looked at me from the front seat, exhausted and confused.

The peace I had on my way back to the airport was indescribable. I was okay. I did what I needed to do, not just for Lauren but for Megan and Nikki too. I thought about the Kingdom, Lauren's Kingdom that she spoke so fondly of. Her kingdom where nobody will hate, lie, belittle, disrespect, hurt, or abandon her. She will be loved unconditionally. *There are crowns waiting for you, Lauren Grace,* I thought. *In your kingdom far away.*

EPILOGUE

THE PAST EIGHT MONTHS have been the hardest of my life. I'm sitting at my kitchen table, watching it snow. *Why do we live in such a horrible place? It's cold. There are no oceans or mountains. It's flat, gray, cold, and pretty much a miserable place to live.* Mentally, I'm not in a very good place.

Lauren has not been doing well. Keeping her at an RTC (Residential Treatment Facility) proved to be one of the worst mistakes we've ever made. I was trying to listen to professionals and ride the wave. Keep listening to the therapists and the school. I will always regret the decision I made when I abandoned my child not once, but multiple times. I was told leaving her was what I needed to do to help her.

I am not locking my child up in an institution because she has a mental-health disease. I thought I could be there to help her through this horrible time, but that's proving to be wrong. Jared and I took turns crying the night we pulled her from the RTC. We did not have a clue what we were going to do, but leaving her there was not an option. Mostly, my heart was breaking for Megan and Nikki, who were going to now be subject to an unknown, miserable home life. I know Lauren's life sucks; it sucks more than any of us know, and it will always suck. I don't know how to help her.

The past three weeks that Lauren has been home have been stressful. Megan and Nikki don't want to come home from school. They don't want friends over; they go to their rooms and don't want to talk to anyone. Nikki's grades have dropped in the last month. I see my girls with no hope for a happy home life. That kills me more that anything else ever could. Jared and I canceled a family Christmas cruise due to Lauren being in an RTC in the hopes that we could go another time. We then planned a little getaway that coincided with a work convention in New Orleans Jared had to be at. We canceled that trip on February 14, as we had no choice but to pull Lauren from the current program she was in and take her home. No money back because it was two days before sail date.

My mom, my dad, and I were trying to come up with a plan for mere survival. They agreed to take Lauren for a week or so every month to give us a break. Lauren went to Florida but was way too overwhelmed. I had to fly down there unexpectedly and bring her home. She was angry, belligerent, and downright horrible. She just couldn't handle it.

Punitive punishment is not okay when you are working with the mentally ill. There is no EBD program, assistance, or para support for us in our district. Nor any kind of reprieve—Lauren has a normal IQ and therefor doesn't qualify for special needs assistance. We feel nobody really cares. People think they do, but at the end of the day, they go home. It's their job. The evening shift and weekend shifts at an RTC are staffed by college kids or people working an extra job with no qualifications to be doing what they are doing. Meanwhile, we spend the evening worrying over when the next shoe will drop and cause an upheaval in our family evening. Lauren's moods are rapidly cycling, probably five to ten times per day. She is exhausted, scared, depressed, and miserable. We won't give up on her. I can't promise that I will survive this, but I will put one foot in front of the other because today is a new day.

As I finished this story from a snippet of my life, I tried to decide where to end. Then I realized that there is no end; life keeps going. Is there a happy, fairy-tale ending? Lauren is not going to magically find friends and skip into the sunset.

This journey is a marathon, not a sprint. I speak to this as a mother who is stumbling through a war zone. Mental illness is a tough obstacle to deal with as a parent, sibling, grandparent, or caregiver. There is no magic wand to fix any of this, and that can be very overwhelming. Lauren cannot escape the reality of the day-to-day torment that she holds onto and can't ever give it away. It's as if she is trapped in her body with a broken mind.

I told this story as a mom, a wife, and a daughter. In all those aspects of my life, I feel as if I'm hanging on by a thread; although, at the end of the day, it's my daughter who is suffering. Not feeling wanted, heard, or understood. Day in and day out, trying to focus and make sense of this crazy world and all the rules she has to follow. "Why do I have to go to school?" In her mind it makes complete sense not to go. She's not able to reason with reality.

Early detection in grade school—seeing the red flags and identifying the problem—was crucial. As Lauren went through grade school, I was bound and determined to keep her issues a secret. I didn't want her to be labeled. She was not going to be different.

Over time, as behaviors got worse, I slowly became okay with letting people know she was struggling. Now, I almost want to put a sign on her back that says, "Back off! I have a mental illness." I made the mistake of trying to keep Lauren "normal." People can be so cruel, and they just do not understand what a parent endures. The looks and comments I get at the store when my seventeen-year-old is having a meltdown really break me down. "She has no control over that child," or, "I would never let my child talk to me that way." Be mindful of those whom you judge, for you do not know what their yesterday looked like.

As a parent with a teen who suffers from a mental illness, I have learned that the small things would make or break my day. I am so overwhelmed at the thought of the phone ringing and school telling me about her behavior. I am nauseated when Lauren is on the phone and I listen to her beg someone to play, or when I watch her on social media and see her face fall when she sees *friends* together without her, truly not understanding why they don't like her.

Mental health issues do not stop with that one person. Many parents and siblings acquire mental health issues as a result of living with and trying to help their loved one. I also struggle with the memories of leaving my child at facilities and dealing with abuse from different schools, and the fear that my life and my other children are going to crumble right before me. I am currently in EMDR therapy. Jared, Megan, and Nikki are all in counseling. We also join Lauren in therapy, family and individual. We battle mental health every day trying to keep Lauren on the right path. The hypervigilance that we have to maintain to feel safe, loved, and at peace is exhausting.

There is no ending. Life marches on no matter how badly you want it to stop. Families that have a loved one who suffers from mental illness just want to be validated. "Do you want to talk?" "Can I take your other kids for a few hours so you can pick up the pieces?" or simply, "Yes, this really sucks. You have been dealt a tough hand, but you are doing all that you can for your child."

When Lauren was born, I had big plans for her, including

creating world peace and a cure for a horrible disease. I can't speak for all parents, but I had that dream. When my child was born, I wondered, *What will she become?* When your child is diagnosed with any kind of mental disability or illness, there is a period of mourning. I am mourning the loss of *what could have been*. It is very difficult to mourn something that doesn't exist. What did I do wrong? *Nothing.* How could I prevented this from happening? *I couldn't.* Am I losing my mind? *No.* Should I feel this way? *Honey, you are entitled any emotion you can muster up.*

I've marched through the murky waters of mental illness. Lauren is home now. She was not doing well at her school, and she is trying to hang on at home. Home is where she wants to be. She wants to be with her family. She is now suffering from severe PTSD, among all the other illnesses. Mental Health Institutions, RTCs, and shorter-term behavioral programs have a place, and I think they can be very helpful, but they can also do a lot of harm. This person is living with lifelong anxiety and depression. All these years I thought I was helping her, but I ultimately caused her more harm—nightmares and memories of what she has witnessed and endured in these schools. She doesn't eat foods that remind her of treatment or wear clothes that remind her of a certain day. Our family is once again in turmoil. I don't know what tomorrow will bring, and that scares me. What do I do, where do I go, and who can help me? Knowing that no one has that answer is terrifying. Knowing that no one can fix this is debilitating.

Tomorrow is tomorrow, and we'll tackle that when it comes. Today, we will march on thinking of that kingdom far away, that fairy-tale ending where all the pain has gone away.

ACKNOWLEDGMENTS

THANK YOU TO MY loving husband Jared and his unbelievable patience, love, and support he shows me. Megan and Nikki, this is tough, but I am always here and will love you forever. Mom, Dad, Katie, Kelly, Nick, and Carol, thank you for the unconditional love and support over the years. It has not been an easy journey. CS, thank you for your friendship. You push me to stay afloat.

Shoutout to NKOTB and the BH cruisers (you know who you are). Such an amazing time together, thank you for making me laugh. Those silly boys and the cruises truly kept me sane.

My Lauren Grace . . . no one ever asked you if this was the life you wanted. Somehow you were chosen to carry this burden and I was chosen to be your momma. We will have great days together and really bad days together. Through all of it, I will be here for you. I love you.

Kari Gusso grew up in Bloomington, MN, and graduated from The Academy of the Holy Angels in Richfield, MN. She received a BS in nursing from SDSU in 1998. She lives in Sioux Falls with her husband, Jared, and her three daughters. Kari worked for many years as a labor and delivery nurse and also worked as a case manager. She and Jared love to watch the girls in their activities, are eager to travel to the beach, and enjoy sitting and visiting with friends and family.